HONEST AS A MOTHER

BOOK 2

HONEST AS A MOTHER: Book 2
Personal Essays That Will Make You Feel
Like You Are Not Alone in Motherhood

2023 LeadHer Publishing
Copyright © 2023 LeadHer Publishing/Amanda Gurman

Art Direction including Book Cover, Typesetting and Layout Design
Copyright © 2023 LeadHer Publishing
Cover Design - Michelle Fairbanks
Editing - Kim Collins
Interior Design - Michelle Fairbanks

ISBN Print - 978-1-990352-70-6
ISBN Ebook - 978-1-990352-71-3

For more information, visit leadherpublishing.com
instagram.com/leadherpublishing

For more information on the Lead Author,
visit instagram.com/honest.as.a.mother

HONEST AS A MOTHER

PERSONAL ESSAYS THAT WILL MAKE YOU FEEL LIKE YOU'RE **NOT ALONE IN MOTHERHOOD**

AMANDA GURMAN

ALINE PADFIELD . ANN MARIE HEMMINGS . ASHLEY TREAVAJO
BEVERLEY BIGGS . BRITTANY BAYLIS . CHRISTIE ROCHA
ELISHA ZAVIER . JESSICA SAWYER . KATIE WICIK
MICHELLE HARRISON-FAULKNER . REBECCA RECHTORIK
ROSSANA SPADAFORA . STEFANIE FERNANDES . STEPHANIE GILES
TOBIE KARST . URSULA ERASMUS . VANESSA DA PONTE

CONTENTS

INTRODUCTION: Amanda Gurman 01

CHAPTER 1: Aline Padfield 04

CHAPTER 2: Ann Marie Hemmings 13

CHAPTER 3: Ashley Treavajo 26

CHAPTER 4: Beverley Biggs..33

CHAPTER 5: Brittany Baylis 39

CHAPTER 6: Christie Rocha..54

CHAPTER 7: Elisha Zavier 65

CHAPTER 8: Jessica Sawyer 84

CHAPTER 9: Katie Wicik...97

CHAPTER 10: Michelle Harrison-Faulkner.................................. 104

CHAPTER 11: Rebecca Rechtorik 116

CHAPTER 12: Rossana Spadafora... 122

CHAPTER 13: Stefanie Fernandes 131

CHAPTER 14: Stephanie Giles 144

CHAPTER 15: Tobie Karst 151

CHAPTER 16: Ursula Erasmus..155

CHAPTER 17: Vanessa Da Ponte 166

PUBLISHER'S NOTE: 177

Introduction
AMANDA GURMAN
@honest.as.a.mother_

Motherhood. The moment most of us wait for our entire lives. We dream about it, hope for it, and wish upon every star until that beautiful day comes when we see 2 lines on the pregnancy test. Then the real fun begins. For nine months, we share our bodies with this tiny person. We eat according to what is best for the baby, we sleep on our sides (wait, did we sleep?), we go to every doctor's appointment measuring their growth and development, and somewhere along the way, it's no longer about you, the mother. I think during pregnancy there is so much focus on the baby that mom becomes second very quickly—so fast that we don't even notice it.

Labour comes, you go through hell to get this baby out of your body, and then the nurse tosses you the baby with this feeling of "Okay, this is all on you now." You go home, and you're in an adult-sized diaper for weeks. You are not sleeping, you are covered in spit-up, and breastfeeding is not at all what you expected. "Isn't breastfeeding natural?" and "I have breasts. Shouldn't I just be able to do this?" you say. You may think to yourself, "Why isn't motherhood coming natural to me like everyone said it would?"

"What is wrong with me?" is the question that some of us ask ourselves.

But it's not us. It's the expectations that are put on us by ourselves, our families, and society. Here's the thing: none of us know what the hell we are doing—not one of us. We are all winging it. Sometimes we get it right, and sometimes we completely mess everything up. Motherhood is a never ending balancing act (that you will never win, by the way). I feel like so many of us go into motherhood with high expectations. We are going to be the best mom. We will breastfeed, we will make our own baby food, and there will be absolutely no screen time. But in reality, we struggle with breastfeeding, we end up ordering pizza (again), and Ms. Rachel is on in the background at all times to keep us sane and the baby from crying.

We make everything black or white. I will either be a good mom who breastfeeds or a bad mom who uses formula. Black or white. I think this is so unfair. Life is certainly not black or white, so why would motherhood be any different? Motherhood is all about finding the beauty in the middle, in the gray.

Like I said earlier, motherhood is a balancing act. There will be days where you will be the most amazing Pinterest mom who does the cool crafts, bakes with her kids, and is fully present. Some days you will be exhausted from these tiny people, and the iPad gets to parent for a few hours while you rest. Both of these moms are good moms.

The most beautiful moments of motherhood live in this gray area. It's almost impossible to find, but I promise it's there. Absolutely nothing about being a mom is black or white. There is no good kid or bad kid, there is no child that always sleeps or never sleeps, and most kids are picky eaters on random days.

This book is going to highlight this wonderful gray area for you. As you read through these incredible chapters, you will notice a theme. Many of these women put themselves in a black or white situation, and nothing turns out the way they think it will. The aftermath of putting yourself into a box is tragic. It leaves you feeling insecure, angry, and resentful. I hope these stories can help you get yourself out of the black or the white and pull you into the messiness of the gray that is motherhood.

Now, when you are in the thick of motherhood and life feels impossible, I want you to remember that you are a good mom. I also want you to remember that you are not alone. This book will also highlight that. Miscarriage, IVF, Postpartum Depression, Racism—these are all very real and very scary topics to discuss, and maybe you will never speak of them, but we will. This book will also normalize the "taboo" topics that come with motherhood. Too many mothers feel alone, like they are the only one struggling. We are all struggling. Some of us just hide it better.

Motherhood sucks sometimes. It's okay to admit that. And if you don't want to, that's okay, too.

Chapter 1
ALINE PADFIELD

www.alinepadfieldcoaching.com | @alinepadfieldcoaching
Photo Credit: Amanda Belec @thirteendesignandphotography

If I am being honest—and since that is what this book is all about: being honest as a mother—becoming a mother was one of the most triggering experiences of my life. Since my daughters will read this at some point, I need to make it perfectly clear to them right from the start that they themselves were not the cause of me being triggered. My childhood experiences became a trigger point as I mothered my children.

Hi, my name is Aline Padfield. I am a mom of two girls, born in 2010 and 2012. I'm a certified health & life coach and the wife of an accountant. And this is my story on how my childhood influenced my life choices, pregnancy, becoming a mom, and other lessons along the way. Truthfully, I am still learning today.

Once upon a time, like many young girls, I had a vision of how my fairytale would unfold. I would find prince charming, we would get married, have kids, and live happily ever after. Well, that is not exactly how it went, far from a fairytale at all. I found and settled for Mr. Wrong, got married, thankfully did not have kids with him, and then got divorced. This actually turned out to be one of the very best things that ever happened to me. Yes, a divorce is the failure I am most thankful for in my life! It allowed me to really find my self-worth. It also helped me to define what I wanted in a partner, but more importantly, what I would never settle for again. First came trauma! There were many realizations that happened for me at this pivotal point in my life. I think it is important to pause right at the start here to give a bit of context on why I picked the wrong partner in the first place and how this would eventually also come to affect who I am as a mother.

Let's talk about my childhood. Childhood is where many experience unintentional trauma. I will not get into the psychology of trauma because I am not a psychologist, but this is absolutely worth learning about because very few people go through life without experiencing some form of trauma. I can, however, speak from experience. Trauma is not just major events like physical abuse or serving in a war. There are many "small t" traumas that aren't recognized in the same way, and their damage often goes unnoticed until uncovered. "Small t" trauma can be defined as an experience that is distressing or disruptive without being physically life threatening.

I came to realize later in life, when I got into my self-healing journey, that many of my basic needs were not fully met as a child. I had trauma. Major fundamental emotional development needs were not met. This was certainly not intentional at all on my parents' part. They did the best they could with what they had. I came from a very loving home, and I never questioned that they were doing their best and loved me very much. In fact, knowing what I know now, I wish they had received more help and support because they, too, were living with trauma. My mom suffered from mental illness most of her life, and that was the reality of my childhood. Regardless of the reason, it does not change the fact that my needs as a child were not fully met. I had to allow that truth to be, as difficult as it was, in order to heal. This had a big part to play in my programming as a child on a subconscious level. These are important formative years. It was not until years into adulthood that I came to understand how exactly that affected me in who I was as a person, my limiting beliefs, my anxiety, and the choices I would make and why. More on that later.

This brief explanation of my childhood and living with a mom with a mental health illness leads me back to why I picked the wrong partner in the first place. There were many red flags from the get go in that relationship. I settled. Unknown to me, I was in survival mode and just wanted to be taken care of and for things to be predictable at any cost, even if that cost was an unhealthy relationship. Here is what I know now and why I settled for that in the first place. You see, my mom would at times fall into a depression that would render her unavailable and, in some cases, hospitalized. In the eyes of a child, having your mom, literally the most important person in your life and your safe space, "taken away" without warning is traumatizing. It is still to this day very difficult to even say that out loud and now put it here on paper in black and white for the world to see. It had a direct impact on my own experience with motherhood, which is what I am sharing about here.

I truly believe that my mom would want me to be a voice for this experience. She certainly did not choose this experience for herself or for me. In fact, I know in my core, being the loving and caring mom she was when she was healthy, that she would hope her story, our story, of motherhood and healing would help someone in some way—to bring awareness as to why we may be a certain way with our own kids, how we feel about motherhood, and why we may be triggered as mothers. My mom got a really shitty deal with mental health and never had the opportunity to be all that I know she could have and would have wanted to be. I got a shitty deal by not having the mom I needed and deserved as a child. That was stolen from me by mental health.

Now I get to heal and spread awareness of those affected by living with someone with a mental health illness. The truth is that many of us are living with "small t" traumas from childhood without being aware of it or talking about it. I see it far too often in my practice. I know deep down that my mom is thankful and proud that I am healing these parts of myself. A woman who heals herself heals her mother, heals her daughter, and heals every woman that comes after her.

As you are reading this, you probably have noticed how I am speaking of my mom in past tense. She passed away from cancer in 2006. When I was around 13, my mom did get properly diagnosed with bipolar disorder and got the help she needed. After medication and education on the illness, she was able to manage her mental health very well for the rest of her time with us. I am beyond thankful for those "good" and more predictable years with her.

I did, however, come to realize when becoming a mom myself just what damage was done from living in a home where mental illness robbed me of a normal childhood. Although not intentional, there was damage. Now I have a bit of an understanding behind why I picked the wrong partner in the first place: I was simply seeking predictability. The most valuable realization from my first marriage ending in divorce was just how important the partner you pick for life is. It is hands down one of the most important decisions you can make. I am so grateful I had a do-over before I actually had kids.

I did end up finding my happily ever after. Here is the part of my story on becoming a mom, with Mr. Right! Then came love, marriage, pregnancy, and loss. Pregnancy did not go as planned, either. I thought I would get married, have fun trying, get pregnant, and—boom—have babies. We got married in 2008. We came to learn that getting pregnant was not an issue for us. Unfortunately, staying pregnant was.

My first experience with motherhood was loss. Miscarriage was a term I became far too familiar with. It awakened an anxiety in me that I had no clue was lying dormant. This experience was devastating, obviously. All the emotions hit me full force. I was sad, mad, disappointed, jealous, downright pissed off, scared, and anxious—and these are just some of the emotions I experienced. But what I learned from miscarriage is how to heal and carry on from it. I had two miscarriages before having my first daughter in 2010. With both of these pregnancy losses, my body knew what to do, and the miscarriages happened naturally.

Some more things I learned from pregnancy loss: 1) It is ok to be mad, pissed off, and angry when you have a miscarriage. Not only is it ok, but it is normal. I remember others around me getting pregnant and having babies with no issues, and I was so damn jealous. I was so crazy happy for them, but deep down inside, I was also incredibly sad for us at the same time. It is ok to be mad and all the other feelings. Feel them; they are valid and normal. 2) If you know someone who has had a miscarriage, do not say any of these things: "It must not have been meant to be," "something must have been wrong," "you are still young; you have plenty of time to try again," or "it will make you appreciate it that much more when it does happen." None of it; don't say any of it. Avoid it at all costs. Trust me, we all know these things, but in the moments of loss and healing, we don't give one shit about any of that. There is no "reason" this has happened to us that will make it better. I know these words are well intended and are meant to comfort, but they likely won't help. 3) Don't ever ask a woman or a couple without kids when they are going to start trying or if they even want kids. They may be trying, and it may not be going well. The actual question itself may be more gut-wrenching than you can imagine. If people don't have kids, don't ask why—period. 4) Everyone processes things differently. Let them heal for as long as it takes. No one can judge what that amount of time should be. 5) Miscarriage is more common than we think. It was not until I experienced miscarriage myself that I found so many women who opened up and shared their experiences to support me in what I was going through. Those women became part of my healing journey. In time, I became part of other women's healing journeys when they had a pregnancy loss. Unless you have experienced it, you truly cannot fully understand.

But here are some things you *can* do to support someone who just had a miscarriage. You know how when someone dies, we make food and bring it to the grieving family as a sign of caring and support? Ya, do that. There has been a death. You may not have known the person or grown attached, but to that mom/couple, they did lose someone, and it is painful. Make them food: premade meals, healthy muffins, fruit baskets, or chocolate—chocolate is always a good idea! Make sure they have easy food to eat because they likely won't want to eat for a while. Tidy up or clean because they won't feel like doing that, either. Just sit with them. Don't try to fix anything or make things better; you can't. There is no fixing this, so don't even try. Get them good books to read and a cozy self-care package with epsom salts and bubble baths. Just care for them in any way possible because they may not care for much for a while. They need that space for a bit to not care and just heal.

And then came baby. Our first rainbow baby! In 2009, we got pregnant with our first sticky baby (as in the first baby that stuck with me to term). When I first thought of pregnancy, I thought of how much I would glow and be so joyful. I thought that I would love every minute of it: the growing belly, the baby kicks, the baby showers, and the pregnancy photoshoots. Don't get me wrong. I did enjoy every one of those things immensely.

However, I think it is important to discuss that pregnancy after loss (or multiple losses) can also be nothing short of gut-wrenching, anxiety-provoking, and a full of fear of the unknown kind of experience as well. I felt robbed of the blissful pregnancy experience because I was always waiting for something to go wrong. I worried all the time. Not to mention, if you think back to the childhood trauma I spoke about earlier, you can imagine all the triggers that came up from that. Things being unpredictable was very triggering for me. Pregnancy was not a completely joyful experience, if I am being honest, and I know I am not alone in that feeling. Not because I wasn't grateful for the opportunity. I was. Not because I wasn't already in love with the baby. I was. Not because I didn't enjoy many parts of it. I did. It was because it was one of the most out-of-control experiences for me. It did not matter how much I wanted it, how much I took care of myself, how much I planned, how many books I read, or how cute my nursery was. The reality of pregnancy for me after two losses was that it could be taken from me at any given moment. That was terrifying.

On March 22nd, 2010, we welcomed our first baby earth side. She was perfect: cute as a button, healthy, and all the things I dreamed of. She was here and safe and mine. I got to keep her! It was sincerely one of the most beautiful and difficult moments of my life.

Now, let's talk about birthing a tiny human with no drugs for a minute. I opted for an unmedicated birth because the idea of doing or using anything that could complicate things or prevent me from having my happy ending with my baby was sheer terror. I had to be in control as much as I could and not give anything the chance to ruin this for me, again. So, natural birth with no drugs is what I did. Holy hell that hurt, and it was one of the hardest things I have ever done. In that moment, I realized my true strength. It was a long 23-hour labour. I pushed for 2 hours, and I am still in awe of what I did that day. But it did not take long for my experience to feel minimized. Enter mom shaming. It starts almost immediately. People may not see it as shaming, but passing any judgement on mom's choices can be shaming. You have no idea how many times I heard, "Why would you not get an epidural? You don't get a trophy for having a natural birth and going through that pain." or "That is crazy. Why would you put yourself through that?" I am not sure if this was an attempt to diminish the accomplishment or make themselves feel better about choosing drugs, but regardless, not cool. We need to do better. How about we don't judge what a mom chooses for herself? How about we consider maybe some decisions are made because there is serious anxiety around the other decisions? How about we just do better and not judge at all? Don't ever tell a mom they don't get a trophy for birthing with no drugs. You don't get a trophy for birthing with drugs, either. None of us do. Truth is, we all should get freaking trophies for it, regardless of the method we bring tiny humans into this world—natural, drugged, c-section, holy it is all amazing! We are all winners. Motherhood and how we do it is not a competition. I think that is where many of us got it wrong. It is not a competition. We are all winners.

Going home with a tiny human that you are now responsible for is something that will test your strength on a whole other level. I did not have a ton of help. My husband is an accountant, so having a baby during the busy tax season was a fun time—not. He was great, though. He was so helpful given he had zero experience with babies. I remember one of the first things I said to him when we had the baby was just how important his role as a dad would be for her. He would be what she will measure all men against later in life. How he treats her and me as his wife will be the measuring stick she uses to gauge how she should be treated. He had a major role to play! And

I'm glad to say he's nailed it, which makes me circle back to my point about the importance of who you choose as a life partner and to have a family with. I am also thankful for my best friend, Michelle, who was not only there in the delivery room, but she also showed me how to give my baby her first bath and answered endless amounts of questions. We also hired help to prepare meals, do some cleaning, and help with the baby so I could rest. We found support because it *is* needed. Don't try to do it all alone. The saying that it takes a village is so true. If you don't have one, build one. Find your people.

And then came the mom guilt! Everything was going pretty well until I quickly hit my first big hurdle as a new mom (enter more shame here, too): breastfeeding. This was my first real experience with mom guilt and not feeling like a good mom. Failing my baby at the most basic level—feeding her. Gasp! I could cry all over again just thinking about it. I did all the things. I saw a lactation consultant, I pumped, I used nipple shields—you name it, I tried it. I was not enjoying it. The experience was starting to crush me. I mean, what kind of mother would I be if I could not even feed my baby? I felt guilty even thinking of trying formula feeding. It was not until my midwife told me "fed is best" that I broke down and said I just could not do it any-more. My mental health struggled, and the level of guilt and devastation I felt was real. We switched to formula feeding. It worked. A huge weight was lifted off of my shoulders, and I was enjoying feeding time as I should have as a new mom. I really bonded with her then. It was beautiful. I was taking good care of my baby, even if it was not as planned.

So this is my take on feeding your baby: do what works for you and don't worry what anyone says about it. A happy, healthy mom that formula feeds her baby is better than a depressed, angry mom that is trying to breastfeed her baby. Now, I 100% agree that breastfeeding is still the best option. I also 100% know we need to stop shaming and judging those that choose not to. Always be kind. You never know what battles people are fighting. Also, remember to be kind to yourself if you are struggling. You are a good mom and you are making the right choices. Trust in that, always.

And then came more loss and rainbow baby number two. So, after settling into parenting and getting the first year under our belt, we thought "We've got this!" Let's do it again. We had a successful pregnancy and a healthy baby, after all. My body knew what to do now. It would be fine, we thought. Like the first 3 times, getting pregnant was not an issue at all. But the anxiety from the first two losses and the pregnancy and the weight of worrying for something to go wrong was right there all over again. Unfortunately, we experienced yet another two more losses back to back. These two losses were harder, if that was even possible. My body did not miscarry naturally on its own like the first two times. It clearly had a harder time letting go of the little beans as well. Emotionally, it was harder on a whole other level as well. It really played games with my mind. All the emotions, all over again! I had a healthy full-term pregnancy and a perfect healthy baby. What was wrong with my body now? Because of my history, my pregnancies were followed closely with several early ultrasounds. We got to see the babies—their heartbeats, their movements, their pictures, all of it. Until one ultrasound revealed no more tiny beating heart. Zero warning. No spotting, no cramping, and no feeling of anything being wrong. It was just a routine checkup and a massive heartbreak. You can imagine the trigger of things changing in a moment's notice and being taken away from me being activated full force. I was in disbelief. Now we had the dilemma of deciding if we would try again. We already had one healthy baby. I was told with every miscarriage, the chance of another goes up. Could I physically or mentally even try again? Well, we did try again. Pregnancy number five went down like number four. My anxiety was high, even though there were no signs of issues. Until I went to a routine ultrasound to find no heartbeat. GASP. Seriously! Again! The question now was extremely valid: could I mentally bring myself to keep trying for a second child or do we just count our blessings with the happy healthy one we had?

We tried one more time, and this baby stuck! Our second sticky rainbow baby! I relived all the same worries and anxieties of my first successful pregnancy, and luckily, it had another happy ending. I laboured for 5 hours and pushed for 5 minutes. Our second beautiful girl was here, and we got to keep her. And just like that, our family was complete! Blessed with two healthy girls.

Now to live happily ever after, right? Well, that is mostly how it has gone. We were blessed beyond measure with success, health, and opportunities to create a life we can be proud of. But I did not realize just how triggering the next many years would be for me, and how, in some ways, will likely continue to be. If I am being honest, motherhood was triggering for me. It is hard to even admit that out loud, still, even with all the understanding I have now. It is still something we just don't talk about. Not out loud, anyways. We need to.

So, as I went about being a mom of two, and as my kids started to get a little older, I started noticing strong feelings of not feeling good enough as a mom. I did not have the most patience. I did not naturally want to do all the things most moms seemed to be doing—the play dates, the picnics in the park, the mom and tot swimming lessons. I was really great at the basic needs like loving, cuddling, feeding, rocking to sleep, and being madly in love with my tiny humans. All the other stuff was not easy, though. I did those things, as any good mom would/should, but there was something off about it. I did not always enjoy it all. What mother does not appreciate this after all the losses?

I would come to learn years later, after a long self-healing journey, getting certified as a health and life coach, and having a life coach of my own, that I was a triggered mother. Many moms have this experience. We just don't dare admit it. It was not until I started opening up about some frustration with my kids around other mom friends and the responses I got that I came to realize I was not alone. I was not a bad mom after all. Other moms also felt the way I did and also did not talk about it for fear of being judged. We all had similar worries. Were we "good enough" moms? Many mothers are triggered and many struggle admitting it. I mean, what kind of mother gets triggered by her own children, right? I asked myself that question often, and you can imagine the judgement that went along with it. Here is one answer: a mother that had a traumatizing childhood.

Triggers come in many ways and for many reasons. If you find yourself triggered in your role as a mother, my advice is to do the work to identify the cause and heal from it. Although this is not easy work, it is work that will set you free from these triggers. It will give you an awareness of why you are the way you are or why you react the way you do. As I continue to learn and heal, I am more and more the mom I am proud to be. I can quickly identify triggers, reframe them, and give myself what I need in that moment. Here is the thing about triggers: they are there to show you something that needs healing. Once we are aware of our triggers, we are able to take better care of ourselves. When we take better care of ourselves, we can take better care of those around us.

In my case, healing my triggers meant re-parenting myself (still a work in progress). My triggers were related to having a bipolar mother. My mom, through no will or control of her own, was not always a present, emotionally available mother. In my childhood, there was unpredictability in my house. Because of this, my very easily influenced young mind started to be pro-grammed, and coping mechanisms were formed. Starting from a young age, I was literally in survival mode. I was always in a fight or flight state, as I never knew what to expect. My nervous system was affected from the get go. On the inside, what was happening to my development was crushing. My programming about myself heavily diminished my worthiness. As a child, when your mom—your safe space, your model, your everything—is just not there the way she is supposed to be (again, through no fault of her own, but my reality nonetheless), it is devastating to your development. I quickly adapted the personality of being strong, just dealing with things, and being "easy" to handle. I never made myself too big, needed too much, or asked for too much. I avoided putting myself in any situation where I would cause stress for my mom or dad or anyone around me, actually, because they al-ready had so much to deal with. I would be good, I would listen, I would get good grades, I would not ask for much, I would not be too loud, and I would not have big emotions that would require them to need to care for me, which would take away from taking care of themselves. That was a lot to process for tiny me, so that is how my coping mechanism was developed. I developed a super impressive skill of being "ok" when I really was (am) not.

Now as an adult, I am a mom myself, and my kids are taking up the space that I was not able to when I was a child, they have big emotions that I was not able to have, and they want and need things from me that my mom was not able to give me—everyday normal wants and needs and behaviours that all kids have and deserve to have. It was triggering for me as a mother who did not have the privilege of developing normally like that in my own childhood. I would actually get frustrated when my kids could not just "handle shit," because I certainly had to as a kid.

At times, I found myself not being present, not because I couldn't be, but almost like I did not know how to be. It was not natural to be present, because I did not have that modelled for me. I was also never able to be present in most of my life, because I was always "on guard" or prepared for the unexpected. I was always in survival mode, waiting for the next unpredictable thing to drop. Motherhood is one big, unpredictable, and beautiful mess that you are never fully in control of. That was triggering. I yelled way more than I care to admit. I did not have emotionally available parents to allow me that space and teach me how to regulate my emotions because, to be honest, we were all fighting a battle to just "deal with it." That was the reality of our situation with a mom (and wife) with a mental health illness. It was hell, honestly. I have never said that before. I say it here because people need to know that this is a reality for some, and it will affect who you are as a person and as a mom.

If my story helps someone identify that maybe they are dealing with unhealed trauma and understand that they are not a bad mom, then my sharing is all worth it. I thought I was a bad mom for a long time. Turns out, I just needed some healing. So, in my journey of motherhood, I have been parenting myself alongside my kids. I say being a mom has been one of the most triggering experiences of my life, but it has also been the most healing. Without becoming a mom, I may have never healed these parts of myself. I am sorry my kids got that unhealed version of me first, but because of them, I get to be the mom I want and deserve to be for them now. I get to do the work. I get to show them what I was not shown. Give them what I was not given. Guide them in a way I was not guided. Support them in a way I was not supported. Be a safe, predictable space for them. Give them room to use their voice, to take up space. Most importantly, I get to show them that I, too, as a mother, am not perfect, and they aren't, either. And that is ok. We are all perfectly imperfect. That has been my most valuable lesson as a mom to date. Be the imperfect mom that you are and model it for your kids.

From the onset of the idea of being a mom, high expectations are programmed into us as little girls. We believe we will mother perfectly, naturally, and without needing help, all while looking good, having perfect bodies, having perfect homes, and having control of everything in our lives. And we will make it look easy. Done. That is your job. Do it. Do it well. Don't complain. Never need a break and love absolutely every blessed second of it. This is a gift, after all. Spoiler: you will never live up to that. Seriously, there is not one dang mother on this earth that hits all those marks—at least not without struggle. I think it is, in fact, critical for the development of our kids that we be imperfect moms. Our kids may be parents themselves one day, and they, too, will not be perfect. What devastation they will experience when they realize they aren't perfect if they were raised by moms that "seemed" perfect all the time.

Many moms make it their job to handle everything, at any cost, for their kids. I would say this is damaging. It's setting them up to feel like failures at times when they, too, have moments of being human and needing support when they can't "do it all." Show them that you need help because they will need help, too. Show them that you have emotions and bad days and good days and everything in between because they will have them all, too. Show them that being a mom is the absolute best thing at times, but you also need breaks away from them because one day, they will need breaks from their kids, too. A really great perspective to consider as a mom is this: Whenever you are judging yourself, being hard on yourself, or not taking care of yourself, ask yourself this one question. Would you want your kids to feel this way or treat themselves this way? Chances are the answer will be "no." If it is, then stop doing it to yourself. If you would not want it for your kids, you should not want it for yourself. It is your responsibility to show them how to treat themselves by showing them how you treat yourself.

Here's my final thoughts on motherhood. It is messy. Much like this chapter, it is not perfect, polished, or well put together. It's kind of all over the place and hard to follow at times. You can imagine the judgement and pressure I put on myself to make this chapter just perfect, but then I reminded myself of the exact message I am trying to send. It is not supposed to be perfect. I am not perfect. Neither are you. Our parents weren't, and our kids won't be, either. Let's stop being so hard on ourselves. More often than not, it is organized chaos that we are all just trying to figure out along the way. Just when you think you have one thing figured out—*bam!*—something else to figure out comes along. None of us are perfect at it, but what I can say for most of us is that we are trying our best, and that is good enough. You are a "good enough" mom.

Let's smash the concept of being a perfect mom, if not for our kids' sake so that they don't grow up with unrealistic expectations for themselves that we know they will never measure up to, but for ourselves as well. We deserve to take the pressure off and be present and proud of how we are doing. If you feel triggered in motherhood, you are not alone. Talk about it, and just be honest. There's no shame. Do the work to heal. Seek help to guide you through it. Your kids deserve a healed mom, but most of all, you deserve a healed you. You will feel immense guilt for not loving every single moment of motherhood all the time. I am here to tell you this again: You are not alone. We all feel the same at some point or another. Find your people and talk to them.

Love and take care of yourself the way you would want your kids to treat themselves. Model it. They are always watching. We may not have received everything we needed as kids, but we get to change that for ourselves now and for our kids. What a gift. Mom, imperfectly, you've got this! Lastly, you are a good mom! You know how I know that? Bad moms don't worry if they are good moms. The fact that you worry if you are a good mom, by default, makes you a good mom—an imperfect, good enough mom. And that is good enough. You are enough.

Chapter 2
ANN MARIE HEMMINGS
@ann.m.hemmings

Dream Chasers

My name is Ann Marie Hemmings. I live in Hamilton, Ontario. It's not a grow-ing metropolis but a city that offers countless resources and life experienc-es for dreamers and enthusiastic people like me: a single parent with an inherent drive to never give up, even when on the downside of opportunity.

My story begins in the early nineties. The Canadian economy was already in a downturn. Even car manufacturing teetered with the threat of mass layoffs. There were more homes on the market in the city than we had seen in years. Mortgage rates plummeted, and it became possible for those who dreamed of such an adventure to be first-time home buyers. I grabbed the handful of letters from my mailbox, sifting through them with derision. Bills, bills, bills. What was I doing? I was a single parent trying to raise a boy into a man. Owning a home was a dream without legs to carry it through to holding the front door keys in my hand. Making it to the major league was my son David's dream. From where I stood, all things were possible, if we only believed.

Saturday morning arrived in a solemn mood. Dusty white clouds sailed in slow motion away from my view near the kitchen window. The West Mountain Baseball season was over, and I planned to wash stained uniforms, wipe muddy cleats, and say goodbye to the first season of baseball. Since I wasn't expecting any visitors, a solid knock on our front door made my heart thump inside my chest. Small feet pattered toward the door, even though I had reprimanded David for his enthusiasm countless times. I grabbed the door handle and pulled it open. David's baseball coach was standing on my doorstep with a sheepish look on his face. "So sorry about this..." he began. When we heard the rest of the news, the pain of disappointment settled in our home like stubborn dust on the kitchen floor. I closed the door and went back to the breakfast table where I watched two sad eyes well up with tears that dripped into a bowl of cereal.

Saturdays were my rest days. No banking issues, no creditor phone calls about overdue payments, and no unwelcome visitors. Those were my weekend policies. Soon after the coach's brief visit, I added another policy to the growing list: no visits from baseball coaches. Kisses on the cheeks and a tight hug that held my boy wrapped in my arms proved to be unsatisfactory, but I offered my support knowing he was deeply upset from the disheartening news. Even though my heart was broken and my mind confused by the discouraging words that were spoken, I remembered the day he hit the ball well enough to score a run for the team. Baseball offered us happy and sad days. I decided to treat them both the same. The end-of-season baseball banquet was that same evening. I had a choice to make. Either I teach him to hold grudges and resent every mistake made for or against him or I wash and dry his uniform and allow him to join his team, fully dressed for the banquet. Some life lessons are hard to teach, especially to an eight-year-old boy. Sometimes our actions are a greater lesson than the words we use to correct or encourage.

The day I registered him to join the sport, I had lofty expectations. The league managers promised to teach the fundamentals of the game, encourage unity, show leadership skills, and mentor the kids in the long-term gains of being a team player. And yes, sportsmanship. Now, after the unexpected visit from the coach, I wondered if I was wrong in choosing this sport for him. Season one showed great promise on the field. The coaches were a group of resolute dads who volunteered their time for the advancement of the sport. They showed up for every game and were intentional in seeing the players do their best while enjoying their summer with the West Mountain Baseball League.

However, we soon learned that baseball was not an inclusive sport, at least not in this league. Or if it was, inclusivity was practiced only on the playing field. But when discrimination and prejudice reared its ugly head at school, I thought baseball would be the playing field of equal opportunity. David made friends on the team, but there were no invitations to develop friendships beyond the baseball diamond. At the end of each game, some of the parents offered their station wagons to transport the "cool kids" going out for pizza, but my kid was never invited. We looked on as feelings of anger and rejection festered in my heart. Looking back, I realize that we could have taken the first step and offered an invitation to come for pizza at our house. But sadly, I was more concerned with how we were treated rather than how we treated others.

I dedicated every Tuesday evening to watching David's baseball practice. I thought it was a good opportunity for the players to gain experience, learn baseball fundamentals, and maybe even make a few friends. Of all the sports available for David's age group, baseball was his sport of choice, his Game of Thrones. On those evenings, before practice, we would toss the ball around at the park nearby. Even when I was tired, it was our routine to do a few rounds of pitch and hit, and we hoped that one day our persistence would give him the chance to sign a major league contract. There were some things I loved about dreams; no one could interfere in our lofty imagination, and the only expense billed to the dreamer was their time.

Thursday evenings held the promise of intense competitions. On those days, my son's uniform was always clean and tucked inside his pants, and he never forgot his cap and glove. We talked about baseball on the way to the games, and then there was even more talk of baseball on the way home. Every swing and miss at bat were recorded in his mind. With vain repetition, he adjusted his glasses before he swung the bat, and whenever he hit the ball hard enough to run from home plate to first base, cheers and shouts would erupt from the parents sitting in the bleachers. Every moment of the experience we shared at the game was met with awe and laughter. The enthusiasm of the crowd gave all the players such encouragement to try again. Run again. Believe again.

The banquet hall was a twenty-minute drive from our home. The coaches had invited the parents to attend the end-of-the season celebration, but it was not necessary. The evening was reserved for the players who showed up to play baseball during the summer months, and even if their team did not win the championship in the league, everyone was still going to be honoured with a trophy. David said it was alright if I didn't go, but I think he actually preferred not to have me there, just in case I lost my composure and spouted uncontrollable angry words I couldn't take back. Memories of season one at the baseball diamond were in the forefront of my mind as I drove to the banquet hall. Even though I found myself crying as I remembered the good moments we shared during the baseball season while I made the necessary turns through the city streets, I also cried to let go of the bad.

Knowing my son would be disappointed at the banquet made my heart sink. As a mother, you would rather hold your child in your arms to shelter them from all childhood trauma and disappointment, but as much as you try, as much as you hold on, there are times when a parent just has to let them know how much they are loved. Then let them go. I chose to stay at the banquet and watched from a seat at the back. I could not leave him there alone. The distressing news did not seem to matter to him anymore when he saw members of his team waiting outside the doors for everyone to show up. There were over a hundred players in attendance. Most of the children came with their parents; others were on their own. All were excited about the fun and food and lifelong friendships they were forming.

As the evening continued, the time came for the coaches to hand out the trophies to all the baseball players. As each child was called up to the front of the banquet hall, their names were announced in alphabetical order by their respective coaches. My chest tightened, and my palms were sweaty. Seeing all the smiles from ear to ear, the firm handshakes, and their walk of pride back to their seats made me smile, too. It eased the tension growing inside my chest as my young son waited his turn for his walk of fame amid the claps and cheers from the excited audience. But the coach did not call his name, nor did he acknowledge that David was even there. However, the name that followed David's on the list was announced, and the young player was honoured with a shiny trophy. I noticed the team members showing off their trophies and talking loudly as they raised them up in comparison to the others at the table. David joined in their cheer, but I could feel his despondency from across the room. Where was his trophy? Where was his prize?

At the end of the procession, when the other children noticed their teammate was not honoured, one of them pointed to David and shouted, "Hey! Where is his trophy?" The coach, noticing the uproar at the table, stood up and grabbed the mic, then faced the audience. He spoke about the great season of baseball they all had and wanted to apologize for the grave mistake made at the end of the season. He went on to express regret to everyone and stated after clearing his throat that out of over a hundred children on all the baseball teams, David Hemmings's name was omitted from the list submitted for a trophy to be made. Gasps of dismay were heard from the parents and other baseball players as the audience went silent. How could the baseball league make such a mistake? When the children heard the news, they surrounded my young boy and offered to share their prize with him. Compassion came in all shapes and sizes. David's grin was wide like the Cheshire cat's; he had made lifelong friends, even in the darkest moments in his beloved sport.

The love of the game was seen in the smiles and hugs of the children who embraced their team member, not for hitting a home run on the baseball diamond, but for showing what sportsmanship meant to all his teammates.

A week went by before I heard a knock at my front door. One of the baseball coaches was standing on my doorstep with a kind grin on his face. He stated how sorry he was over how the season ended, but he was proud to see this young boy rise above it. He handed me a shiny trophy as I shook his hand and nodded with thanks. David's dream of playing in the major leagues had been tarnished, but not broken. It continued to live on simultaneously beside my dream of owning my first home, a dream I had dared to believe although it seemed impossible.

I had saved up ten thousand dollars with the intent to spend it on a once-in-a-lifetime dream vacation. David had his sights set on a new mountain bike or a cruiser skateboard—anything with wheels he could flip over at least once. I often took him on short weekend getaways to theme parks with hopes of exhausting some of his energy. Meanwhile, I continued to add to my savings while I dreamed of a Disney World vacation. It was going to be a marvellous two-week adventure: four days on a Disney cruise and six days at the Disney theme park in Florida. I wanted the vacation to be near the end of the summer, just before he went back to school to start a new year. Every night, instead of reading Dr. Seuss, David wanted to skim through the Disney World brochure once or twice. We planned our activities around the grand event which was but a short three months away.

A few weeks before settling my plans with a large deposit to the travel agency, I made my weekly visit to my mother's house. I sat down with a cup of tea and told her how excited I was to take this dream vacation. I had been saving for the trip for five years. Her reaction surprised me. She was reluctant to endorse my ideas. She encouraged me to wait before I gave my hard-earned money to a travel agency. She thought all the money I had saved should be used as a down payment on a property that could produce a tangible long-term investment. I knew she was right, though my stomach tightened as if I had eaten liver and onions for breakfast.

I left my mother's house feeling discouraged; I had always trusted her judgement. She stood by me when I was pregnant and alone after a few months spent nurturing the wrong relationship had left me with an uncertain future as a single parent. My mother often encouraged me to pray. She said the answers would come if I prayed. That night after I left my mother's house, my aunt called me. She was one of my closest friends; we often spent hours on the phone talking about our life experiences and our hopes for the future. This time, she had good news to share. She had found a perfect starter home for her family and was thrilled to tell me that there was one on the same street that would suit me and my small family. "Ann Marie," she exclaimed. "Your uncle and I just bought a house—our very first home! You've got to come see it! And I think there's one available for you, too."

"What! I cannot afford to own a house," I said. I believed in a young boy's desire to pursue his dream of playing baseball, but owning a home was much more difficult than hitting a home run out of the park. Besides, what about our Disney vacation? I hung up the phone and quickly called my mother. Before she could say hello, I was already asking gruelling questions. Did she hear about the house on the market that I could afford to buy? Did she think I could be a homeowner? I remembered her telling me to think long term rather than just enjoying the moment. But I had made a promise to take my son on an amazing vacation. The time away would be a sweet relief from the pain of the baseball fiasco we had endured. Now my aunt had presented a proposal for another option—a better option, perhaps? But who was to decide which choice was better? All proverbial fingers were pointing to me, the mother, the decision-maker, and the one carrying the heavy weight of raising a precious child on her own.

Later that night, I tossed back and forth, kicking the crumpled sheets off the bed. I was frustrated, knowing I had a heart-wrenching decision to make. Should I make great memories on a two-week adventure or take on a mortgage for our very own home instead? In time, I calmed down and took the time to pray for direction and wisdom. I even skimmed through the brochures. Any kid would love the four days on the cruise, making new friends, going on treasure hunts, and swimming in the refreshing pool. David had cutouts of the Disney vacation brochures taped on the wall in his room next to posters of his favourite baseball heroes.

I thought of how my mother raised her three children to be strong individuals, enduring the storms and the good times of our lives with the same attitude. She was not afraid to make sacrifices for us. I had seen her make enough choices that required her to be as hard as steel in her determination to see her family thrive. She always said owning your own home was better for your future than paying rental fees every month. I knew her advice made good financial sense. And eventually, it would help my family to prosper.

My two brothers owned homes of their own. I was renting a two-bedroom townhouse and was content to do so. Until now, buying property was not on the table for at least another two years.

I awoke the next morning with a new curiosity to see the house. I called my mother and asked her to come with me. She had a wonderful friend who was a real estate agent who agreed to accompany us. It was the old stately neighbourhood that caught my attention—landscaped properties and well-equipped sports parks. This would be a fresh start that we would both love. It was a three-bedroom, semi-detached house with a huge backyard, enough space for a garden for me and lawn enough for a young boy's antics. I cried when the tour was over. I knew then that we would not see Disney World for an exceptionally long time. My mother held me in her arms, allowing me to cry freely. "Thanks, Mom," I said. "You were right."

While having dinner would have been an opportune time to deliver the bittersweet news to David, but the roast chicken tasted extra crispy, and the baked potatoes were doubly good. While we watched the Blue Jays baseball game may have been a better time to share the news, but the home runs were numerous, and we shouted with cheers at the TV instead. Then it was his bedtime. My heart was heavy with apprehension, but I could not put it off any longer. I sat down on my son's bed and began to tell the tale from the beginning. My mother's advice came to mind. He may not understand now, but later, he will understand.

Chapter 3
ASHLEY TREAVAJO
@ashleypick33 | @ashleyt.mortgages

Women are expected to work like they don't have children, but raise their children as if they don't have a career.

Mom guilt. I believe every mother can relate to those two words, no matter what stage of motherhood they are in. We feel guilty about what to feed our children, to breastfeed or to formula feed, what type of school and/or daycare they should go to, and the list goes on. Another big mom guilt that we all have had is over the decision to return to work or be a stay-at-home mom. This last one has had a huge impact on my life and where I am today professionally. I feel like in my short 5 years of motherhood, I have been in almost every position of the working or not working mom debate.

Before I became a mother, I had a career that I loved and had major aspirations for where I pictured I could go. I worked in frontline healthcare as a physiotherapy assistant and occupational therapy assistant (PTA/OTA) in some of the biggest Greater Toronto Area (GTA) hospitals. I LOVED my job. However, I felt like I had hit my ceiling very fast. As far as medical professions of the world go, I got to do and see some cool things, from walking with a ventilated ICU patient, working with organ transplant recipients, and assisting with legacy work in palliative care. These were all really amazing opportunities and just a handful of highlights in my career. I went on to get a bachelor of health studies (BHS) and a postgraduate certificate in gerontology. I had major goals to get into managerial positions within various healthcare institutions. In fact, I was actively applying to new positions up until I found out I was pregnant with my son in February 2017. I stopped applying to the jobs that interested me and actually turned down a few interviews, as I knew before becoming pregnant that it would be a high-risk pregnancy. Plus, I didn't want to add more stress to an already stressful and unknown world that I was just embarking on as a first-time and high-risk pregnant woman. Also, at that time, I was working in a long-term care facility (LTC), and my job as a rehab assistant was quite physically demanding. Again, I just didn't want the stress and anxiety of job hunting while now being put on job modifications at the nursing home.

Fast forward to July 2018, and we had just moved into our first home! It was so freaking exciting to start this new journey. But we had literally been in the home for just 3 weeks when I received a phone call from my manager at the LTC facility, while still on maternity leave, saying that my hours were going to be changing when I get back to work. My guaranteed 25 hours a week (which is great when you're making $30 an hour!) were going to be cut down to one shift a week. I was devastated and started thinking, "How the hell can I contribute to the household on only one shift a week?!" *insert mom guilt*

I finished my maternity leave in September 2018. While adjusting to daycare pick-ups and drop-offs *insert more guilt,* I started actively looking for a new job. I started a new job in October 2018 at a medical equipment store. I actually liked aspects of it, but I missed my LTC job. I was trying to get into the groove of this new job environment, but the daycare illnesses kept coming, and on top of all of it, my son and husband got into a car accident on October 31st, 2018. I had to take so much time off from October to December that year. I felt terrible—terrible that I was letting down my family and terrible for letting down my new employer. *insert more guilt*

At the end of November, the owner of the store pulled me aside into her office and closed the door. She sat there (a mom herself, too) and asked me if I am the one that will be taking time off from work all the time whenever my son is sick. My stomach just dropped, and I wanted to cry. How the fuck do women do this?! How can we be a good mom and contribute financially to the household AND have our own goals and aspirations and feel fulfilled career-wise?! *insert *all the damn guilt**

On December 23rd, 2018, I gave in my resignation letter for this job I had for not even 3 months in fear that I was going to get fired anyways. I decided to go back to the LTC home and take my one shift a week on Saturdays and be a stay-at-home mom (SAHM) during the week. Woah! What a damn whirlwind those few months were for this first-time mom who was so anxious about returning to work! By working the Saturday shift at the nursing home, I felt like I was still able to contribute financially and was able to hold on to my career that I worked so damn hard on. But on the flip side, I was experiencing more guilt that we only had one full day a week to spend together as a family of three. In hindsight, it was the best decision we could have made. This whole being a SAHM during the week allowed me to finally enjoy being with my son and doing all the fun mommy things that my undiagnosed postpartum anxiety and depression robbed me of in his earlier months. I felt present and loved all things with my son for the first time since he was born. Don't get me wrong, it was a shit ton of work being in that role. In fact, it was one of the hardest jobs I have done. I took it very seriously and even had my own version of Montessori school with him in the early years. I think we all needed that time. I felt like we were in a great routine. We finally had a great thing going! We loved the daily and weekly activities, and I actually felt somewhat fulfilled by spending time with my son and working on Saturdays.

April 2019 rolled around, and I had a positive pregnancy test in my hand. All I could think was, "Nooooo! Not yet!! We finally have some equilibrium in our lives!" So there we were again with another high-risk pregnancy, this time trying to keep up with a toddler and working Saturdays. I lasted about 6 months and then was off on sick leave by October 2019 due to cardiac issues I was having. Baby girl was born at the end of January 2020, and we were trying to adjust to life with a newborn and a toddler. I felt ready to get out to the mom groups, activities, and all the events in March 2020, but … Well, we all know what happened then. Welcome to the shit show.

April 2020 rolled around, and life was crazy with the pandemic. I was getting updates from colleagues about a COVID-19 outbreak at the nursing home, which ultimately led to the deaths of 50 residents. I was on the sidelines healing and raising babies while all of this was hitting the nursing home I had been working at for the previous 5 years. Residents I knew and loved were passing away. It was extremely hard and surreal to be seeing it all un-fold on the news each day. I was also in such a postpartum fog, and I thought why not add more crazy to an already chaotic situation? I had been thinking about a new career for awhile. I was intrigued back when we bought our first home by the two professionals that helped us get our home, the realtor and the mortgage specialist. I registered for a mortgage agent course, read the text on my phone between nap times and nursing sessions, passed my exam, and became a licensed mortgage agent in September 2020.

To say jumping into the entrepreneur life from a completely unrelated pro-fession has been a learning curve is a major understatement. I went from swiping a time card in and out, asking for approved time off, reporting to managers and therapists, surrounded by others all the time (as healthcare is a 24-hour business, after all) to now being self-employed where it's just me, myself, and I. I am the one responsible for finding and keeping clients, and I am responsible for my own pay cheques and how much money is com-ing in. I report to myself. I have taken it upon myself to find a village within the mortgage community to help me be accountable for my success. It also takes a village to raise a new mortgage agent, and I am very grateful to those that have made this transition a little bit easier and not so lonely.

And, you know what? I am not the only mom that has made a huge career shift during the pandemic and definitely not the only one to do so after be-coming a mother. I see and hear of so many women that, after becoming a mother, have had to give up on their career dreams and goals. We get into this motherhood thing and realize that life in the 20th century is not what it was when our own mothers and grandmothers were raising kids. Now, don't get me wrong. I am in no way saying life was easier back then. Many of these families were uprooted to flee countries that had wars, depressions, and poverty. Technology was nowhere near what it is today, which helps us stay connected with the world. But one thing I truly believe was better back then was the village. That saying "it takes a village to raise a child" was very true back then. Now we see multiple generations still alive and working in one family. For example, my grandmother was alive up until 2 weeks of me writing this. She passed at 92. My mom has been retired for the last couple of years but was the primary contact and caregiver for my grandmother. Then there's me and my children. We have these sandwich generations that can't be everything to everyone. Another big difference is how difficult it is now to have a family on just one income. Again, I'm not saying it was easier years ago, but it is crazy how much rent or a mortgage is, plus with inflation, everything is just so damn expensive. This is why so many women must return to the workplace after maternity leave—to keep up with the bills. And not to mention, unless you have said village to help with childcare, you have a daycare bill on top of that, too!

So with the lack of village and rising bills, moms are heading back to work with their kids in various forms of childcare. But what happens when a mom must take time off because, God forbid, their children get sick or they have an appointment. Or what about her? What if she needs time off to be sick or for appointments? We just don't feel like we can stay on top of all the torches, which at times are all on fire. In my situation, I left one job because I was afraid of getting fired (I guess my pride thought it was better to quit before they let me go for being off so much with my son). But why should it be like that? Why are women forced into this guilt every day of deciding what is more important: the career they worked so damned hard at getting or raising their babies?

And let's address the pandemic and the mental and physical load on women. Women held the homes together during the pandemic (Shout out to the men out there, too. You also need acknowledging, but this is for the mamas). We saw women running businesses and sticking with their careers while their villages—for some it was family, for others it was childcare centers/homes—all fell apart. There was no daycare, no families, and no schools to keep their babies safe, looked after, and educated. These women did it all! But let's not reward them for doing that. Let's take this as a lesson in how society needs to help and pick these women back up. They are tired out, stressed out, burnt out, and feeling defeated. They have felt all the repercussions of momming and working all in the same physical space. I have done that for the last three years, and it is so hard. In fact, I have now secured an office space outside of my home because I get so distracted with all things housework and kids, and I need it for my own mental health, too. Many of these women have had to leave careers they quite possibly loved, just to keep afloat in the house. Or some, like me, have made huge career changes that would be better suited to family life. For me, that was becoming an entrepreneur, which has its own challenges and tribulations. The pandemic has allowed the world to see how much mothers all over the world are willing to do to provide the best for their families. But it has also shown the world that we are, in fact, still a marginalized population. Gender inequality still happens in many homes and workplaces. Women are still getting paid less in many industries, all while doing the same work plus home making and child rearing. The pandemic has taught us so much, and one big lesson is that women, of all races, religions, and creeds, hold this world together.

It is now January 2023 at the time of me writing this. Our society seems to be getting to a more "normal" way of living post pandemic, but many of us are still reeling and recovering from the last few years. We are running on empty in so many aspects of our lives: mentally, physically, emotionally, and financially. Women have been working, raising and birthing babies, creating and growing businesses, all while trying to practice self-care (what even is that anymore?!). We mamas are burnt the fuck out! There is just no other way to explain this feeling that something else is going to happen in our worlds, and we are constantly on guard, waiting for the next crisis and the next pivot we must make. Many of us are putting off our goals and dreams while we are raising young children and living this pandemic life. But if the last few years have taught me anything, it's that life happens. No matter what is going on in our personal lives or in the world, each day moves on. Sometimes it feels like one day is actually 72 hours, while other days speed on by. But another huge lesson I have taken out of the last few years is learning just how strong a mother can be to hold the household together.

Really, what I want you to know, dear reader, woman, and mother, is that you should go after those goals. It doesn't matter how crazy, big, or scary they are. Life with kids makes you feel like there is always something going on—appointments, sicknesses, sports, school council meetings, growth spurts, and on and on. But you matter, too. Our goals and dreams are what fires us up. It's ok if your first pathway to a career hits a dead end. Maybe that rocky path has all the signs that lead you to a career/lifestyle that fulfills you mentally, professionally, and personally. If you want to be in a corporate career, do it! If you want to be a stay-at-home mom, do it! Or maybe you want to turn that side hustle into a small business full time. Just do the damn thing, girl! Find the people and resources that support whatever decision you make. There may be stages in our lives where we do put things on hold (in my case, while I was dealing with two high-risk pregnancies), but those stages do end. There is light at the end of the tunnel. Just don't sit back in 40 years wishing you had started that master's degree or business or applied to your dream job. Moms, we *can* do it. It's not easy or free, and it looks different than that of our male counterparts, but we are capable. We *can* feel happy and fulfilled as moms and, if we choose, career women. Our children are watching us every day and taking notes. As a mom of a boy and a girl, I want them BOTH to see how important and valued women are, not only in the home but in the workplace, too.

Shoot for the stars, girl. You got this!

Chapter 4
BEVERLEY BIGGS
@beverley.biggs

Everyone starts out by picking a profession, and then we all go through the struggles to make it work. Everything comes together, and you are finally feeling comfortable with where you are. You feel that you have mastered your first chosen profession, or at least to the best of your abilities. THEN, whether it's planned or not, you find out you are pregnant! It's glorious news! A new little person is coming into the world, and he or she is going to be calling you MOM! You are entering another new career, and that's when it begins: that feeling that you are not doing everything you need to or you're not meeting all the societal expectations, and everyone is giving you advice because they think they know what's best for you.

When it's a first pregnancy, you have no idea what changes are happening to your body and how it's going to react to these changes. You're not sure what exactly needs to be done and if you are doing right or not. You are fearful that you are going to make mistakes and feel guilty when something doesn't go as planned. The desire for perfection and to be the "perfect mom" is all you can think of. There are so many things to think about, and all you know is that there is a wonderful little human growing inside you that is going to make you a mother.

This is my experience of becoming a mom and how I have learned to deal with societal expectations, family and friends' expectations, as well as my own expectations. I had a career I loved, I met a partner, and I began making plans with him. We had just purchased a house together and settled into living under the same roof when we discovered that we were expecting. It was wonderful news, and we were both thrilled by this unexpected twist in the plans we had been making. It was at that point that I started to question myself on everything. I considered myself a normal person, but was I even doing things right? I was keeping everything to myself and trying to make sense of it while also trying to hold a strong front that I knew what I was doing. I, like many others, had a strong exterior but was questioning everything and holding it all inside. I basically bottled everything up and wouldn't let anyone see how many bottles I was keeping.

Once I found out I was pregnant, there were just so many first experiences for me: prenatal doctor's appointments, morning sickness, and still managing to work at my place of employment through it all. Coworkers began giving me suggestions and offering me support to help me continue working throughout the pregnancy. It's all a new learning experience, and all the guilt starts immediately. There is still a desire to have a morning coffee, but the doctor says to cut the caffeine. Cutting some things is easy, others not so much! Pre-pregnancy, I lived on coffee!! I compromised and had one coffee a day. But was this ok for the baby? I was second-guessing myself, but I had my doctor's reassurance that I was doing ok. Just as I was finally managing being pregnant, it was now time to start thinking about delivery.

Due to many issues, my doctor sent me in to be induced at 39 weeks, and any thoughts of a normal vaginal delivery were shot within an hour of being there! It turned out I was allergic to the inducing cream. We found out the hard way, and I ended up with an emergency c-section! As I reflect back on it, I have regrets. I never got to experience childbirth. My experience was not what most women experience; it wasn't normal. I had to learn to accept that my experience was just that—my experience! But I never experienced the natural delivery process that I had hoped for and was expecting. So this is another mental jar on the shelf of bottles to be dealt with.

I can honestly say that I did not have a difficult baby. My son was happy as long as he had a clean bottom and a full tummy. I was very lucky not to have many of the issues that so many moms (and dads) have to deal with. But even with how good he was, I was still questioning everything about what I was doing or what I chose for him. Was I using the right diapers? My body wouldn't produce milk, so I had to use formula; but was it the right formula? I was lucky enough that I had a very supportive husband, and he reassured me on everything that I questioned. It made it easier to continue and do what I needed to do. That's one thing that I hope everyone has—a good partner to help you deal with the many questions and issues, maybe alleviating the need for the next mental jar. I had taken maternity leave from work, and that year just flew by!!

Next was figuring out who was going to care for my child while I was back at work. The choice of staying at home was not an option. Our household was used to having and needing two incomes. So back to work it was, but before that could happen, I needed childcare! The question of home daycare versus a daycare center was an easy choice because at the time, we didn't know anyone that ran a home daycare that we both would trust with our child. So daycare center it was—but which one?! The choice became clear when we found one that could accommodate our needs. And the staff were all great! But the biggest guilt I have ever felt was that first day of leaving him crying in a daycare worker's arms!! The caregiver was amazing and just kept saying "Mom, he'll be fine!" I remember it as if it was yesterday. Walking away was such a hard thing to do! The daycare worker was right, and it became easier as the days went along. But the anguish of going back to work and the guilt of leaving him was hard. And looking back, choices were made, and I dealt with everything as it happened. I still wish that I could have had more time at home with him, but you can only take the amount of time that the government and/or your employer gives you for maternity leave! Needless to say, life moved on and there were many more instances of doing the mom things every day only to have issues pop up where you question yourself as to what you are doing and why.

Finding a work/life balance, as they call it, wasn't easy! My Supermom cape was sometimes in the washing machine, and I had to put on my big girl panties to deal with stuff. The morning rush to get out of the house, having a sick child, and trying to clean the house, all while Mom also had other places to be and other things to do, was chaotic. This balance wasn't easy. My son inherited his mother's clumsiness. So before he was even 5, Mommy had taken him 4 separate times to get stitches. And when he was 7, he decided to try out a new set of monkey bars at the back of a school. That ended with a cast on his arm from above the elbow to below the wrist! All of these things, Mommy wasn't around for. They happened at daycare, school, aftercare programs, or out with others. I was working and had to leave unexpectedly to deal with the issues. Guilt set in—that if I had not been working, I could have been there. But quite honestly, I can't have my child walking around in bubble wrap. And looking back, I know that he needed to learn and grow as his own person, just as I was learning to be his Mommy!

But I tell you, those were some pretty big mason jars that were getting bottled up! As he was going through school and participating in activities, I was thrilled to be able to see what he was learning and how he was growing or developing. I, however, was not always able to be present for everything. So again, guilt set in for those things that I couldn't make it to. But with some very understanding managers over the years and a good bank of vacation days, I took every opportunity I could to spend as many school trips, parties, or awards ceremonies as I could with him. I didn't want to miss any of them, even though I wasn't always able to be there.

Now the big one! Think back to February 2020, and the world has shut down because of the World Health Organization's declaration of a worldwide pandemic!!! An unknown disease has made its way into the human world and is making its way around the globe rapidly. COVID-19 was shutting things down, and requests were made for everyone to stay at home in their own little household bubble. Well, this Mom couldn't do that. I was a healthcare worker and was declared an essential worker! With both of his parents declared essential workers, where was our son to go?? Everyone was cheering us on and saying we were heroes, but we were also Mom and Dad, and decisions had to be made. We asked around; no one was willing to take our kid, as they feared the unknown of COVID-19. But the expectation for us was to report to work. Thankfully the YMCA (and yes, I am giving them a plug and a round of applause for this!) stepped up and created a safe place with some of their staff that our kid could go to and be taken care of while we worked. Even though this was all put into place, and everything was working quite well, I personally still had a lot of fear and guilt about leaving him under someone else's care and going into the hospital to work with COVID-19 patients. The unknowns existed for me, too! I feared bringing it home. I wasn't sure what the other kids in my son's room at the YMCA may have or bring in. Many unknowns were out there, and it took the longest time to settle into working with COVID-19 and figure out how to protect myself and my family from getting it. Life had to go on, and through many circumstances and waves of this disease, we managed. And I managed—but not without putting some more jars up on the proverbial shelf of bottles!

Living up to the world's expectations that a full-time worker/full-time mom can do everything was hard. But even harder was living up to family and friends' expectations—and even my own expectations! My proverbial shelf of mental bottles or mason jars existed quietly in the background, and trying to be this "normal" mom that everyone saw me as... it was hard to deal with them sometimes. I kept them to myself and trudged through things. Looking back, I learned so much from everything as I trudged through. And I had to learn to deal with those jars. Sometimes it was easy, and sometimes it was hard. And even now, some of them are still up on that shelf to be dealt with. But we have time... I have time!

So what have I learned? Being a perfect mom doesn't make you a good mom. Trying to be a Supermom is next to impossible—but you can still have the cape! Work/life balance is just that—a balancing act. And we are still working on it, no matter what age we or our kids are! Having a good partner is a must!! You can do it on your own, and some do, but there is a reason why it takes two to make a child: it takes at least that to raise them—so ask for help! Taking care of oneself is sometimes the best way that you can take care of others. We are all going to have regrets and times of guilt, and many mistakes will be made while being a mom. We are only human ourselves.

My biggest lesson: open up those proverbial jars, remind oneself that it's all now history, and learn to let it go! I don't need to hang onto everything. I have learned from them, moved on, and am in a good place to just keep going!

Chapter 5
BRITTANY BAYLIS
@baylisb | IG: @love_forlearning
Photo Credit: Cindy Csordas Video Production

It is when we are down that we discover what we are capable of. It is not the easy days that build us into what we desire to be but the challenges that enable us to get there.

As we embark on this journey together, it is my true hope for you, hand over heart, to walk away with tools in your toolbox. I am going to walk you through my journey, with some of my lowest points, and share how I was able to shift my mindset to help me change gears. Over time, I learned to embrace the struggle, to find my inner strength, to persevere, and to become stronger. For me, this was in relation to motherhood, stemming from the anxiety of trying to conceive, to the losses of miscarrying, and to the fear of losing a child when there was too much uncertainty. Finally, I will take you through my NICU journey and explain how this trauma came to be and how this pain was transformed to become gratitude. For me, gratitude is the memory of the heart, and my heart will be forever impacted and changed by my experiences. When we learn how to convert pain to positivity, we can begin to enlighten ourselves. We have to tolerate the rain in order to fully enjoy the rainbows.

What is the rain, exactly? It is the darkness. It's the moment when we begin to lose sight, when we get caught up in the overwhelm or get lost in a belief that isn't true to ourselves. Sometimes we aren't even certain of what that really means. Life isn't easy... it's not meant to be. The more we resist, the more it persists. Visualize what you want to happen, accept what is, and use that energy in your thoughts to think about how to get to what you want. It's in the difficult moments where our decisions can get us closer to our true selves. If we are able to correlate suffering with the climb, then the grief of losing becomes an awakening.

My first miscarriage brought me to a state where I felt I had lost control. I automatically went inward and blamed myself. The whole dialogue had a negative tone. "What's wrong with me?" My heart ached because everyone around me who was getting pregnant either didn't want to be pregnant or got pregnant with ease. As I sat with the anger and pain, I reflected and tried to figure out why this time got me so low. What was I attached to? It was a belief... but was it even mine? In my mind and heart, I had created a timeline and a set age when I had to accomplish specific life goals. One such life goal was that I had to have my kids before 30. Why 30? This ideology enabled me to feel stuck. That's right. My own idea of what should be was causing my very own anxiety. Month after month, I created my own sense of disappointment. There would be a two-week window of hope, crushed by the first sign of blood. I would analyze, scrutinize, and judge my every thought and symptom, then cross-reference it all on Google, ultimately creating more angst and further emphasizing my failure of meeting my life goal.

I was in this space where life would stop. The awareness was huge. That's why we sometimes stay there. The story replays, and we are so far down the rabbit hole that we can't get out. I realized that I had put all my happiness into one thing: becoming a mom. With this high expectation of conforming to a societal timeline, the pressure in turn created perfectionism. I felt like I needed to control everything for the stars to align. I was losing sight of my vision because I was so caught up in the day to day. I was timing intercourse to a point where it became an item on the to-do list. I was losing sight of the journey. Once I became aware, I was able to refocus my attention and concentrate on other things. I slowly dabbled back into other passions, so I had less time to concentrate and focus my thinking back on this one thing. I brought back the joy and the true meaning of being present. I developed cross-curricular programming where my class created costumes, designed music, and put on a play for our school assembly. I fell back in love with the arts.

When we learn to let go, life surprises us.

I remember that feeling like it was yesterday. When I saw the two lines, I felt a vivid sense of full-bodied overjoy, a "scream-off-the-rooftop" kind of vibe! As soon as you venture into visualizing, your body and mind truly experience it as if it is real. I was already three steps ahead, visualizing the pregnancy, the baby, and my life as a mom. But, I do also believe we have instincts for a reason. I knew something was wrong. I remember hearing the doctor say in his cold tone that this baby wasn't going to make it. Time had stopped. The grief was raw. Was I allowed to feel a loss for something and someone I never knew? In my heart, I was already connected. I find when things go south, we are the first to blame ourselves. When we face failure, we find guilt, blame, shame, or anger instead of self-compassion. We need to speak to ourselves from a place of love like we would for a friend. I needed myself to be my best friend at that time. I needed someone... anyone. Instead, I closed the door and turned off the light. I spent some time in solitude. The grief began to heal, but it did not release.

Connection is why we're here. It gives us purpose and meaning.

I knew I had to reach out, talk, share, and make sure I wasn't alone—or at least didn't feel that way. A deep grief made it hard because I had days where I did not want to talk. In fact, it was easier to be alone. *However, it's in the vulnerability where real change happens.* I knew the fastest way to reset my mood was to shift my energy and bring kindness back into the world. I knew I could reset by being kind. *We reflect the energy we put*

forth. It did not have to be big. A simple "good morning" could change the tone of my day, leading me to send a message or spark a conversation. When we pause, we are able to really determine what our heart needs. Meditation builds our mental awareness. It's key to everything. **Notice and name. If we can name it, we can tame it.** I was sad, disappointed, and fearful of my future.

A few months later, the second miscarriage was not any easier. The pain was still so real, but this time, I knew I needed to advocate for myself. I needed to get specific in advocating for and understanding my needs. I laid it out there. My heart was breaking, and I needed answers. The doctors referred me to a fertility clinic. I believe that things happen for a reason. I was in the process of gaining fortitude. Control, perfectionism, and anxiety were present as well as a heightened sense of fear. Finally, I was pregnant! I believed that this was my time.

It was going well... until it wasn't. I started feeling back pain—like deep, intermittent pain. I remember that drive over the Skyway Bridge. It felt like an eternity. I was breathing heavily through unbearable pressure and overpowering lower back pain. The warning bells were going off as I started to hear my thoughts. I kept ignoring them until I no longer could. As the doctors were doing a routine check, nothing seemed routine. Many people were coming in and out of the room. Finally, after moments of uncertainty, they explained to me that I had an ectopic pregnancy. The baby was stuck in the fallopian tubes and would not survive. I had a choice to make. I could go to their other clinic an hour away to get a cancer drug or I could rest at home and try to process what was happening. We chose the latter. I was in shock and denial. I still had hope, even after they told me. I was in disbelief. Not again... this can't be happening. I made the decision to write my supply plans. Within an hour, as I was writing, the pain hit. I was hurled over. It got so intense that my shoulder had a sharp stabbing pain. I called my family to inform them. They didn't even know I was pregnant. By the time I arrived at the hospital, I couldn't keep it together. I was vomiting; my response system was kicking in. The medical team took my vitals, and many people rushed in. My clothes were cut off within seconds, and the lights and the faces were intermittent. As they rolled me down the hall, I truly felt that everything was over—that my chance of being a mother, my hope of having someone to play with, to love unconditionally, and to grow old with would cease to exist.

Nine hours later, they managed to control the bleeding. I was in surgery for hours upon hours. After a few transfusions and because of an incredible medical team, my life was spared, but I was left broken. Physically and emotionally, I was scarred. I could see the scar of a c-section, yet I had no baby. Fear took over, and I started to google my prognosis. I felt a deep sadness. I wanted to hide or wake up from the nightmare. I was grieving all over again. Was it anger? Fear? What was keeping me hostage? How much time is enough to grieve? I read blogs of women's success stories, I reached out to professionals, and I began my soul searching once again. I needed to know how to keep my faith alive. **Oftentimes, it is a simple decision that can change your life forever**. Will I keep fighting? How much do I really want this? *When we fall, it's how we get up... and continue... that defines us. Life only throws at you what you can handle. Sure it's not fair, but you have a decision to make: use it to learn and be better or play the victim and stay stuck.* I still believe it was my fight and my destiny. I connected and took time to heal by being around loved ones.

Suddenly, I received a call to hear that my older sister was in labour. Excitement took over, and without hesitation, I was there by her side. This was a turning point in my path. It was an "a-ha moment," if you will. Being there for this magical beginning was exactly that. It was another realization that we don't have control. This is bigger than us. Witnessing this miracle sparked and healed my mind and heart all at once.

Moments in time line up, if we can just have enough patience to wait.

I had that glimmer of faith, but I knew I couldn't move forward alone. I needed a bigger power than me. I needed something to guide me when times got tough. I needed something I could hold onto. Through conversations, I learned that the local church had blessings on the first Sunday of every month. If you were expecting or hoping to conceive, you could be blessed by a Father. I found myself attending these blessings regularly, and they helped my thoughts stay at bay. Finally, I had another chance! I was PREGNANT!

Hallelujah! Was it too early to celebrate? I was afraid to say "I'm pregnant" out loud, for fear it may not come true. Once I crossed the first finish line and moved into the second trimester, I started to breathe. I felt a sense of relief. I knew I had to keep my mind strong, so I turned to literature. I fell in love with *Magical Beginnings* by Deepak Chopra. It was beautiful, and I wrote regular journal entries to my unborn child about my feelings, sensations, hopes, and dreams as I felt them. I recognized that I was having moments of imbalance where I felt negativity had snuck back in. This time it was an old problem, one that relates to body image.

What people think of you is none of your damn business.

We spend our lives at the mercy of the scale, trying to lose weight, and here I was watching the scale climb. I knew that this was part of the process, but when you're pregnant, it is now "socially appropriate" for people to comment on your weight. People feel that they can touch your belly and ask how much you've gained, talk about your glow or acne, and really lay down what they really think. "Enough," I say! I have fought for this, and I'm not going to be robbed of all my joy because of someone else. I fought these thoughts on a daily basis. I bought the next size up and embraced it.

The moment I longed for—anticipated, visualized, dreamed of, and de-sired—arrived. It was August 28th, and Ayla was born!!! The labour was long, exhausting, and excruciatingly painful. I was induced, and the contractions were on top of each other with no breaks, but I had triumphed. I couldn't stop holding her... staring at her... life was grand! She is my perfect little dolly, precious to me. I took pictures of my pictures, I dressed her up, and I googled ways to stimulate milestones. We went to an infant massage session and attended baby Picasso classes. I wanted to experience everything. I knew I wanted many kids, so I made the decision to try again. This time I was *that* person. I was the one that I had envied. I was pregnant at my first attempt. Talk about disbelief; I was astonished.

Ayla was just 9 months old, and it was hard. I was sicker than sick, but in the same token, I was happy to be sick. I felt a sense of overwhelm. My energy couldn't keep up with my responsibilities. My work was demanding of my energy, especially with an hour commute each way. I was teaching kindergarten with a one-year-old when my oldest fear returned... blood. I was blessed to work with the doctor who saved my life, so I went back with that same look in my eyes, asking for answers. The doctors could not find a reason. It wasn't reassuring. In fact, it gave me more stress. The blood continued, so they determined bed rest was in order. Bed rest with a one-year-old?! I think not. I started to feel squirrelly. I was organizing socks and cleaning the grout, nesting at its finest. After a few weeks of bed rest, I started to have waves of gas pains. My husband was at a hockey game while the pains were happening, so I soaked in a bath. I tried to sleep, but by midnight, I was awake. All of a sudden, I needed to get up and start moving. This helped for a short time, but then I knew I needed to get to the hospital. I took a cab, and by the time I was coming down the escarpment, I was swearing and started to have to focus on my breathing to get through the pain. Once I arrived, they checked for dilation and discovered I was at 6 cm! They told me to call my family. This baby would be arriving soon. Talk about disbelief; he was two months early. The pain got intense fast. My husband arrived with only seconds to spare, as at that very moment, our son was born. I got a short second of skin-to-skin connection with my baby before the shock, joy, and worry exploded in my heart and my brain. And that's where the real journey had begun.

Did all the other things happen to build me up for what was in store? Seeing my baby attached to all those cords, watching his vitals, and being on edge all the time was intense. Every time there was a beep, I was terrified. There wasn't a time during his hospital stay when I didn't wonder if there would be a tomorrow. Will he make it through another night? Just being in that room exposes you to traumas that will permanently impact your heart. Once again, I could feel my mind being toxic. Fear and anxiety were at the forefront. I couldn't stay in that cloud. I needed to find the energy to move me.

All it takes is a shift in your mindset to change your perspective.

I turned to what I love: music. **Music is therapy.** Music is a way to release my emotions. I also wrote how I felt, so I could be in the moment. "No one knows what it's like to be waiting, always anticipating the worst. No one knows what it's like to feel so much love and not know what to do!" Singing validated my feelings and allowed me to refocus on seeing the mini milestones. When I finally got to hold him, the tears wouldn't stop flooding. Once he no longer needed the CPAP, we found out the colour of his hair. When you look for positives, you train your mind to see them.

Because of the people I met, the relationships I formed, and the habits I created, I started to feel at peace with all of this. I often spent the day with my daughter, and after supper or once she was in bed, I spent the night at the hospital with my son. For 9 months, I pumped every 3 hours. I was just happy he was alive and that I could hold him. My fears started to dwindle. I felt like the days were catching up with me, and being up all day and night was taking its toll. So I took one night to get some rest, with the intention of heading to the hospital in the wee hours of the morning. But that night, I was awakened by a dreadful call. My son was in distress. He was non-responsive and needed to be transferred immediately. They believe he had developed NEC, which I learned is a potentially life-threatening stomach condition. Seeing his lifeless body on a stretcher and inside an incubator hooked up to so many machines left an imprint I will permanently have in my brain. I kept it together the best I could, but once I gathered the knowledge I needed, I screamed and cried. What did this mean?! Had we come this far to have it all stripped away again?! What should I do?

Carter arrived at Sick Kids Hospital, and every 8 hours for 8 days, we were on surgeon watch. The surgeon met with us, reviewed his prognosis, and determined the course of action needed to keep him alive. I felt a sick, nauseating fear constantly taking over my body and my mind. It was an overpowering sense of doom. My thoughts were creating stories, and my ability to manage day to day was slipping. I needed to get my control back. I had to let all this out. I wanted to scream, but I knew there was more I could do.

My husband and I celebrated our 30th birthdays (our birthdays are only a day apart) while Carter was still in the NICU, so we invited our friends and asked everyone to bring donations for the Ronald McDonald House. We used this space to re-gather ourselves, to pause from life, to connect with others, and to listen to other people's journeys. This experience gave us the strength to keep going. Our newborn son gave us the strength to keep going. He fought through this tough time, and he taught us to believe. No more code pinks. No more holding my child in my arms as he turned blue while I called for someone—anyone—to help!

Everything is temporary.

You just can't give up while waiting for the darkness to pass. Trust me. I needed to say it, sing it, hear other people say it, and repeat it several times before I allowed myself to believe it, too! The light started to shine bright, and finally I could see a better road ahead. My daughter turned 18 months and got all her shots, which meant she could finally meet her brother. On St. Patrick's Day, Ayla got to meet Carter. After that, more weeks had passed with success, and we got to bring our son home!

Many emotions were at play: joy, worry, shock, and so on. The days went by fast, but the weeks did not. Carter cried all day and all night. He was colic for most of his first year. I felt like I tried everything. Being outside sometimes helped, and gripe water or football holds just bought us patience to hold it all together a little bit longer. It was hard. I had a hard time admitting it, but I felt guilty for wanting my own time. Did this mean I was not a good mom? After all, I wanted motherhood more than life itself. I waited for that break when my husband came home, except he didn't come home at set times. He worked in the golf industry, which meant late nights. He was gone all day and sometimes late into the night. He always came home, but often by the time he walked through the door, it was too late. I was asleep, and the kids were asleep—for the time being. Month after month, my husband and I became more distant, more like roommates or business partners. We drifted apart. We didn't have time to talk, to share parts of our day, or to really be involved in each other's lives. I didn't really notice this was happening. I fell back into meditation to help myself cope with the increasing demands.

When we quiet the mind, our soul will speak.

We have the answers, if we are patient enough to find them within. We have to be able to ask the right questions. What do I need? What makes people successful? Routines! An ebb and flow. I needed something to look forward to. We found out about a literacy center nearby, and we developed some beautiful friendships there. I met my current daycare professional there. I trusted her because I saw how she was with the kids day in and day out, and I knew I wanted someone who would listen to, encourage, and love my children in a nurturing way. I struggled with asking for help because I felt it meant I wasn't capable. I fought hard for this privilege of motherhood, therefore, it was my job as a mommy to do it and do it all. Was fear somehow involved in this, too? I remember someone saying that *it's ok to ask for help because it gives you freedom to do more.*

When we are developing a new skill, we need to start small. We need to take mini steps, pause to reflect, and then continue to take on a little more. I began with asking the teacher to watch the little one while I took the toddler to the washroom. I was afraid to be dependent on anyone because I knew I needed more faith in myself. I learned that the best way to achieve this was to do it and to find ways to love doing it. I was slightly addicted to Pinterest. Maybe that contributed to me becoming a recovering perfectionist. I loved watching my students' and my own children's faces light up as they discovered something new. I'm blessed to be a teacher so that creativity is part of me. I couldn't really separate from it. I would look for ideas on the fly. What I did learn quickly is that you need to be filled up as a mama. If you want to embrace the chaos and paint with yogurt, you need to have slept or have had a good cup of coffee. Otherwise, the mess might throw you astray. If coffee and sleep fail, resort back to music. Music is a mood changer. Put on your favourite song or find one that matches your desired mood and play it loud and proud. Dance it out, play, laugh, and be one with the moment.

I truly love playing with my kids, and so when it seems like we're off course, I know it just means we need to reconnect. Get outside. Be one with nature. Roll down the hill, and jump in leaves. *Embrace your inner kid.* This is another fast reset trick to change course. Having this gift, to be home with them, was simply that—a gift. Saying goodbye to the time at home was hard. Was I making the right choice to go back to work? Did it make me less of a mother? I was constantly torn and ridden with guilt. I would cry on my way to school and be so tired on my way home.

I wondered how long it would take for me to get my groove back. Weeks flew by, but my confidence wasn't where it once had been as a teacher. I second-guessed emails or decisions and always asked myself, "*Am I doing enough?*" There were certain things I couldn't do anymore, and it all came back to time. The guilt of being away from my kids and the guilt of being home with my kids and away from work when they were sick was difficult. Sometimes I felt like I was failing on both ends. I had to find the balance, and I had to keep enough energy for both areas of my life. Once I felt I had achieved this, I was ready to begin another journey into motherhood.

The agony was repeated, and the fertility journey pushed our limits once again, but the busyness of our lives made it less of a strain when things didn't go as expected. A year had passed, and we were blessed again with another opportunity for another magical beginning.

"The more you read, the more you know. And the more you know, the more places you will go." I knew I had to open that book again to build my mental capacity. I re-read Chopra for the 3rd time. I started a new journal for my unborn child and began to connect once I felt safe to do so. Some fears may never leave you. Is it fear, or do we have boundaries to protect ourselves? Either way, I arrived at a safe spot again and began to share the news. This time, my care was transferred to a perinatologist. There were many more appointments, which meant extra time off work. And that added to the guilt and stress of being a working mom. But still, I knew it was better than what I experienced previously.

Then, at 33 weeks into my pregnancy, the fear returned. I was hospitalized because I had a slow leak. My water broke, but luckily it was a slow leak, which delayed the arrival. It was yet another hard time as a mom because I had to leave my two younger children at home in the care of their father and my mother-in-law, without their mom. I remember my mother-in-law bringing my children to visit, and instant tears fell from my eyes as they came off the elevator. I felt a guilt that I had somehow failed them. I couldn't be there for them. Was there something wrong with me?! I couldn't go there. I knew what "there" was, so instead I found joy in the little things.

They released me from the hospital but warned me that if my cord comes out, I was to go on all fours and call 911. Another week had passed with daily stress tests, and the decision to induce labour was made. Labour isn't always what we claim it to be. I'm afraid to say this "out loud," but Phoenix's birth was a victory. It started off with light cramping. I walked around the corridor for hours. I even got into a rhythm where I had a good pace going and felt a sense of accomplishment. Active labour changed the tone. I was restricted to the bed, but it only lasted a few hours, and by now my body had been conditioned. The waves were peaks and valleys, but there was rest in between for me to be able to get my bearings for the next round. Six hours had passed since the onset, and by the afternoon, I was holding my newborn son! Phoenix was born! Within a week, we were home. And within a few days, we were back in a routine and finding ourselves at the center again with our parent community.

We need to find our higher purpose. It is our goal to walk into a room and make it a better place.

Play was a vital part of our day. I found my excitement was contagious. Watching and facilitating their growth and development was my mission. Making sure they felt nurtured, stimulated, and loved made me feel complete. Getting used to three children took some time, but my oldest was now in school. How did this time go by? They don't prepare us for when our babies grow up. Time truly goes by fast when you're having fun.

But then the sky had darkened, and the rain cloud was back. Phoenix started looking sick. He was losing weight and refusing to eat. We brought him to the doctor's office and were immediately referred to McMaster Children's Hospital. He was admitted for several weeks in search of the cause. Many tests were administered with possible outcomes that had haunted our thoughts. Will our son survive? What will happen to him? Phoenix's weight loss was significant; he weighed nine pounds at nine months old. Panic, guilt, and blame were all back and fully loaded. Persistence, grit, and hope overturned and triumphed over fear. I surrounded myself with positive energy.

Our diet is more than our food. It is what we watch, who we surround ourselves with, and how we spend our days.

Finally, Phoenix was released with an NG tube, and we were trained how to medically feed him for the next six months. It consumed us. And when he pulled the NG tube out, it was an ER visit. Once, he pulled it out three times in a 24-hour time period. Our trips were based on how close we were to the hospital because he was dependent on consistent feedings. I was back to pumping to supplement. Once again, we were building our capacity and opening our hearts. **Don't let the nightmares have more power than your dreams.**

Time had healed my heart, and I was ready for one more chance at creating a new life. Deep down, I really wanted another girl. We mentally prepared as much as we could to head down that road again, and low and behold, it was rockier than all the others. Being faced with another ectopic pregnancy crumbled me in a new way. I miscarried for months, but the worst part was that I had to go for blood work every other day to determine my fate once again. Will I lose my other fallopian tube? That would mean in vitro fertilization for me, and the anxiety was back because I knew how close to death I could be. Was I selfish for doing this to my family? Leaving them without a mother? Darkness was upon me; it surrounded me.

Knowledge isn't free. You have to pay attention.

My mind needed virtue. It needed to be repolished and tuned up. I decided to put the work into myself. I spent time studying meditation and the science of happiness at Yale and Leiden. I read, wrote, and became part of what I was learning. The biggest truth is that we have power over our thoughts. If we can learn to recognize negativity when it first arises, we can breathe it out of our system before it has time to stir up stories. The Calm app is a resource I still use daily to reset, refocus, and recharge. Everyday, we need to unlearn and retrain the mind to build capacity. No one is immune to this.

When my daughter finally arrived, it wasn't without tribulations. In fact, my body was so used to this process, that it messed it up even more. For 9 days, labour started and stopped. I was stuck at 6 cm dilation, and half of my body and face went numb. A team of doctors and specialists, including internal medicine, rushed in to prepare me for the possibility of a stroke, but luckily enough, it turned into complex migraines instead. This is another challenge I face, but I do believe these are all building blocks in my capacity for life. Grief of all these losses proved to me that love will return in a different form. Ariel's arrival consolidated all my pain. It transformed my suffering into key learnings that I'm blessed to share with you.

Our failures are our pathways to our successes.

When we lean into the hard, we come out stronger. My aunt once said, "the more things we go through in life, the better people we become." What does that mean? It all boils down to empathy and experience. We can connect, relate, understand, and grow. Awareness is the foundation of all of this, for we need to know how we're feeling and how it's impacting us to be able to figure out the next course. Being a mother has hard moments and moments of pure joy. Life has taught me many things. It's taught me to slow down. Being busy stops you from enjoying what's right in front of you right now. It's hard because it's a fine balance of routines and keeping children engaged but also to allow them to be bored. Go with the flow and see what they need at the time. When we have nothing to do, it allows us to embrace what IS rather than rushing to get to the next thing. Do what feels right at that moment.

Self-care isn't selfish. It is a necessity to build patience. For me, exercise is non-negotiable. If I work out, I build my patience so that I can take on the interruptions, spills, messes, meltdowns, and unpredictable occurrences with minimal disturbance to my mental state. If I don't take care of my body, a small thing like not being prepared can shift my mood. I find any form of activity is key. **Move every day.** Dance, run, lift, or swim, and the more you enjoy it, the more it becomes a habit. If it interests you, it will motivate you. Do things that get you closer to who you want to be.

Teach them how, and you will give them the gift of being able to teach someone else.

Sometimes it's "faster" to just do it or show your love by having it all ready for them, but if we can teach them, it builds their confidence. And if we are confident, we can do anything. Lastly, learning to listen and wait is a life skill. Hearing what people have to say and giving your time is an honour. Sometimes we lose sight of this because we're thinking of a response. Waiting is a constant in life, just like change. When we don't know what to do, we do nothing. Time heals many wounds.

Be aware of what you need and what your children need, and do your best to pair them. Try to include learning in all that you do. Make math part of casual talk and have them communicate often in various ways. You know that look on their face when children are really engaged in something? Do things to spark that. If you love what you do, you can do more.

And if all else fails, get outside and be one with Earth. After all, we're all in this together. We are all on borrowed land, so choose wisely.

Chapter 6
CHRISTIE ROCHA
https://sasssays.com/ | @sasssays

"I have to tell you something," I confessed to my husband. I had spent the last hour talking myself through all of the reasons why I was absolutely NOT attending my sister-in-law's Zoom birthday party. It was August 2020, my family, along with the rest of the world, was 5 months into the COVID-19 quarantine, and my head felt like static radio. "I can't fake a smile. I don't want to talk. She will understand," I convinced myself as I bathed and dressed my kids for bed. In my family, birthdays are a big deal, especially when we haven't seen each other in months. I knew I couldn't physically show up without also being mentally and emotionally present.

My 2-year-old daughter and 6-month-old son were finally tucked into their cribs when I went about my nightly ritual of crashing face down into the white, fluffy pillow at the top of my bed. I'd lie there for however long, re-viewing the day and dreading the next, feeling lifeless, numb, and whatever the next-level word for exhausted is. This ritual marked the end of the gazillionth long, mentally challenging, repetitive, isolated, and draining day of entertaining, caretaking, cooking, housekeeping, feeding, and wiping.

I felt depleted of everything I needed to exist as a human being. Raising little ones while completely isolated from common support systems like babysitters, daycares, family members, libraries, and play centers was unimaginable. For a time, even playgrounds were off limits. And yet, here it was, imaginable and happening.

Eventually, I'd talk myself into the next step in the ritual: a shower. "Shower and see how you feel," I commanded myself. A shower was like a palette cleanser. I shampooed, conditioned, and scrubbed away the day. This time, I also ran through the speech I planned to deliver to my husband about why I couldn't celebrate. The scalding hot streams of water atop my head and down my face were almost meditative. Months before August 2020, a shower was all I needed to kick the static radio feeling, but by this point in the lockdown, it only temporarily muted it. After my shower, still up in my room, I heard my husband singing, laughing, and pouring drinks at the kitchen table. I was late to the party I wasn't going to, but I got dressed and thought, "Ok, just go down there, wave hello, say happy birthday, and tell J (my husband) that I'm not feeling well, and I can't stay."

So, that's what I did... sort of. The universe works in wonderful ways. I did exactly as I said, and immediately following my brief appearance, the birthday girl shared that she needed to end the call for 15 minutes and come back. I believe wholeheartedly that happened for the exact reason I needed it to. Everyone exited out of Zoom, and I stood frozen, staring at my husband. "I have to tell you something," I said. And to my surprise, he put one of his hands on each of my shoulders, looked me in the eyes, and said, "I know." He caught me off guard, but not really, because he tends to read me like a book when I least expect it. In fact, now it almost catches me more off guard when I don't anticipate him reading me like a book. Anyway, I arched back in surprise, but out of necessity, I quickly dropped my shoulders to a sulk and said, "Well then if you know, can you just say it?" My head fell, and I stared at my socks. Somehow I knew he really did know. He wasn't guessing. He knew what I hadn't yet accepted. "No," he said. "You have to say it out loud." After a long pause, I confessed, "I think I'm depressed." He hugged me close and whispered, "I know."

What neither of us knew in that moment was that it would propel me into the life I have now and the person I am now. Today, while very much still a work in progress, I have a life. Period. I experience joy. I seek out and find pleasure in activities, people, and places that, for a time, did nothing for me. For me, depression didn't manifest as sadness; it manifested as devoid of feeling. I loved a thrilling crime show, a juicy *Real Housewives* moment, a compelling podcast, a walk outside, and great food, but seemingly out of nowhere, these things meant nothing to me. There was nothing I looked forward to. I couldn't think or sleep, and yet I never wanted to move. Lying down in the darkness suddenly felt like the closest thing I had to a "happy place." I would never have imagined that almost exactly one year later (to the week) of that confession, I would launch a podcast about mental health and therapy advocacy for women and moms called *Sass Says*.

Prior to having children, I had never experienced depression. Like everyone, from time to time, I knew how it felt to be sad, down, low, and I'm sure even depressed at some point, but never like this. Never day after day. I had heard and read about depression, clinical and postpartum, the way one might hear and read about space travel. I know it's out there and it's happening, but not to me. I'll never experience space travel or know what that feels like, so it exists in my mind as an almost-theoretical concept. Knowing what I know now, it's mind-boggling. When I was a child, my mother, grandmother, and great-aunt taught me *The Silva Mind Control Method* by Jose Silva. They brought me to seminars and raised me to be self-aware and interested in what makes people tick.

By the time I was in high school, I learned that I was actually interested in what my family had taught me, and I wasn't just doing it because they wanted me to. I loved astrology and psychology, and I considered studying to become a family therapist in college. Unfortunately, I got it into my head that the only way to be a successful person, which, if you are familiar with the millennial American dream story, means that you have to "make a lot of money." And in order to "make a lot of money," a person should go into a field known for achieving just that—think accounting, finance, insurance, medicine, law, etc. Long story short, I tried accounting and hated it. I transferred programs within my school, graduated, and took a job completely unrelated to my sociology and English majors, which I eventually very willingly left when I had my daughter.

From a young age, I was interested in and had a light pulse on mental health, psychology, and the mind/body connection. I was an athlete, a softball pitcher, and my father taught me all about mental fitness and how my emotions had an impact on how I physically threw the ball. And yet, as an adult, I couldn't fathom that I could have postpartum depression, that I was allowed to see a therapist, and that medication was a perfectly acceptable treatment option. I couldn't fathom that in becoming a mother, I'd experience so much emotional pain. And I really couldn't fathom that from that pain, I'd embark on an incredible healing and self-development journey that I am still on today.

One of the main pillars of my podcast is that you can always count on me to ask, "BUT HOW?" "Take care of yourself," they say. "Put yourself first," they say. "Self-care is important," they say... BUT HOW? How do we actually do it when as mothers, our time, attention, and energy are divided up amongst many different people and responsibilities. And to that point, I bet you're wondering, "So how did you go from depressed and immobile to writing this chapter?" And I'd love to tell you.

Therapy & Medication: So I already told you that I didn't think therapy was for me. And not because I didn't believe in it, but because I literally did not know I could go. I always wanted to go, truly. I was deeply intrigued, but it was one of those theoretical concepts like I mentioned before. I understood therapy to be for someone who was suffering from what I refer to now as a "big T" trauma—think divorce, death, illness, abuse, and so on. For much of my life, I believed I didn't have any problems—not any real ones, anyway. I thought of therapy as inaccessible and a last resort. I also naively thought I'd be taking a spot away from someone who really needed it. I simultaneously want to smack this version of myself in the face with her condescension but also give her a hug. She, like everyone else, I believe, deserves therapy.

How I Started Therapy: Pregnant with my son (my second child), still griev-ing the very sudden passing of my other sister-in-law, mothering a toddler, and grappling with what my life had become since leaving my job, I found myself in an uncomfortable place with my lifelong friends. I was upset about a NY Giants football game, of all things. The details aren't important, but basically I was in my feelings about who was going, when everyone was clued in on buying tickets, and who was sitting with who. You don't know me or my friends from Adam, but this was preposterous and completely out of character for me. I chalked most of it up to pregnancy hormones but still vented about it to my mom. I could hear in her voice how much she wanted to tell me to snap the hell out of it, but she kindly humoured my turmoil. I shared my pregnancy hormone theory with her but also shared that I just felt sad about the whole thing, to which she replied, "Ya know, Chris, just a reminder that you can always call me when you're in your feelings, especial-ly about your friends. Those girls are like daughters to me, so I don't take this all to heart." Through tears, I blurted out, "Mom, I can't call you every time I feel like this, every time I feel sad, because most of the time, I don't even know why I feel sad. Sometimes it's just because it's Tuesday!" That was her clue that perhaps I needed a professional.

A day or so went by, and my mom came to me with some mind-boggling in-formation. Her friend, Sara, shared on a podcast that she simply went onto her health insurance website and found a therapist. Therapy was covered by health insurance! Say whaaat, now? She added, "And ya know, Sara re-minds me a lot of you. She is happily married, has beautiful children, and is building a business she loves, but she goes to therapy to hash all the things out." And honestly, that was it.

I went onto the Horizon Blue Cross Blue Shield website, found behavioural health, scanned through the names and photos of the therapists, and picked one that looked like me. She doesn't actually look anything like me, but she looked like someone I know, someone I could relate to, and luckily for me, she is my same therapist today. She is the best friend I know next to nothing about. I owe much of my healing to the work I've done in therapy. And if you're wondering what "the work" means, well in my view, it really just means kindly calling yourself out on your BS. It means asking questions, reflecting, and trusting your therapist to be your guiding light and sounding board. My main takeaway thus far is that my feelings, reactions, perceptions, and thoughts are all that I need to examine and nurture. Period. I could go on and on about therapy, and I encourage you to listen to my podcast where I do just that!

After a year of therapy, I figured out that the stigmas and misconceptions I had, and that many out there still believe, about therapy are false. Medication, however, took a little longer to wrap my brain around. I won't lie; medication terrified me. I was afraid of becoming addicted to it, of overly relying on it, and of the shame and the feeling of being too weak to take care of myself without it. These fears only reveal to me now how little I knew about it and how much I was letting societal messages dictate my life.

On a Thursday night, following my nightly ritual and within a week or two of my depression confession, I caught an Instagram live with Erin Washington and Michelle Dempsey-Multack. I had worked with Erin back in my twenties. She had recently written a book on recovering from an eating disorder and finding balance in motherhood. And I knew of Michelle from Instagram. She is a podcast host, author, and divorce coach for moms who I loved, despite not having been divorced. Within the conversation, they spoke about anxiety and revealed that they take medication for it. I heard two women, one of which I know in real life and another that I've revered for years, on Instagram talking about medication, and something shifted. Now, suddenly, everywhere I went (figuratively, of course, because I was locked down in my house), everywhere on social media, television, and podcasts, I'd hear about medication—specifically, antidepressants.

When I brought it up to my therapist, she thought it was a good idea to explore it as an option. There was part of me that wished she had recommended it sooner. The other part of me recalled my internal reaction of, "NO. NO WAY. NOT ME" when she disclosed months prior that she needed antidepressants while pregnant and postpartum. Funny how that is, huh? The stigmas around mental health and medication, particularly for postpartum moms, are still alive and well. I learned that not only are they damaging and false, but that they were impacting my life—not some theoretical person's life out there somewhere on a spaceship but MINE. The messaging around motherhood, that we are built for doing it all, is harmful. We need help, real help. I needed to get it through my thick, "all moms are superheroes, so what's wrong with me?" skull that getting help in motherhood does not make me weak. Remember this: Therapy and medication are forms of help that have shown me how incredibly strong, capable, and truly badass I am. I am your evidence.

More Than Mom: All of the above is what ultimately drove me to start my podcast. Not knowing therapy could be for me, learning so much about medication and how it works, and wondering why more people weren't shouting this from the rooftops prompted me to say, "Ok, I'll shout it!" I always knew I had something to say in this world, but I could never figure out what it was. I had a blog in college, mainly about my dating escapades, that fizzled out once I found happiness with my now husband.

I had a transformative experience at a Taylor Swift concert in my mid-twenties. I recall watching Taylor as if I was taking notes for my future self. This is embarrassing to admit, but throughout the entire concert, I was internally begging her to GIVE ME THE MIC. I desperately wanted to be a person who impacted people, who had something powerful to say, but I could never quite get a handle on what I cared about.

I remember getting back from a walk with my first baby and googling, "how to find your passion." Once again, I want to laugh at this version of myself but also hug her. I knew that a Google search wasn't going to get me anywhere, but I was desperate. New motherhood didn't feel magical, Pinterest-y, or even enjoyable much of the time. I wouldn't have phrased it this way then, but I had completely lost my sense of self. In every way, shape, and form, life as I knew it was unrecognizable. That being said, I am grateful for whatever it was inside me that prompted that Google search because with each new search, personality test, and self-help podcast episode I listened to, I got a little closer to launching my show.

I'll spare you the nitty gritty of how (as in all the individual steps I took), which goes against every fiber of my being, but I promised to tell you how launching my podcast took me from depressed and immobile to where I am now. And simply put, my show reminds me that I'm more than Mom. I have a name. I have ideas. I am smart. I am worthy of really amazing conversations and relationships with the women I interview. Back when I started my podcast, it gave me a sense of community, especially during a time when virtual communities were all we had. And still today, my community continues to grow. I have met incredible women and moms who indirectly fulfill me and give me purpose just by showing up, but they also directly influence my real, non-spaceship-y life.

Whether the interview is about marriage, postpartum mental health, body image, productivity, or parenting, I am learning something new every episode. I am growing emotionally, intellectually, and spiritually with every interview. Pretty cool, right? My podcast is mine, for me, for you, for moms, and for women. It gives me a sense of purpose outside of motherhood. I highly recommend this for moms at any stage of the journey. It doesn't have to be a podcast—it can be painting, jogging, or killing it at a job you love—but I promise you, as much as you love your kids, you need something that's yours. And just to push you on this one more time, even if you are or plan to be completely fulfilled by curating the perfect bento box lunches, themed birthday parties, matching outfits, and playground visits, one day your kids will grow up. They will need you less and less. And yes, I am shooting it to you straight here, stabbing at those heartstrings, but you either work to find yourself now or you will have to find yourself then. Remember this: Rediscovering myself, what I value, and what I want to say in this world makes it possible for me to deeply and meaningfully enjoy motherhood. I am your evidence.

Treat Yourself Like a Newborn Baby: Speaking of finding and rediscovering yourself, I need to address self-care. I know. I hate the term, too. It's overplayed. Forced. Annoying. Meh. But it's necessary, especially when you are depressed and immobile. You already know how society suggests women and moms to do self-care: manicures, shopping sprees, massages, and girls' nights out. I will ride for all of these things, but as a new mom, a quarantined mom, a working mom, whatever kind of mom you are, these things just aren't accessible, possible, or achievable on a regular basis.

Join me for a moment in the theoretical space above our foreheads and picture two chalkboards, cute ones with adorable lettering, something you'd see at a coffee shop. One chalkboard is for the "here and now" self-care habits, and the other is for "big picture" self-care habits. I had to learn and practice the "here and now" habits for, admittedly, years before I could incorporate the "big picture" habits. Here are some examples of "here and now" self-care habits (write them down on one of your chalkboards): deep breathing, drinking a glass of water, eating, moving your body, calling a friend, listening to music or a podcast while doing dreadful chores, keeping up with your doctor's appointments, and taking a rest when your body calls for one. Incorporating these habits while depressed and immobile felt impossible to me.

Depression was a vicious cycle of knowing what I needed to do but having my body and brain telling me that those were the exact things I was totally incapable of doing. It's messed up. Every week in therapy, I shared my goals to walk, to drink water, to eat, to sleep better, and I can't say there was any one thing that made the difference as to when I incorporated them, but slowly over time, I did. I want to emphasize *slowly and over time*. I also want to validate you if you are where I was, knee deep in depression and immobility. These habits sound SO easy, but I know there are times in life when they feel as difficult as climbing Mt. Everest. I see you. My advice is to take one step, to do one tiny thing at a time. If you want to drink more water, start with one more sip than yesterday. For me, this was gruelling and, at times, absolutely infuriating. But I have the experience now to know that each sip starts to add up, and you'll wake up one day and find that you're drinking a gallon of water without even realizing it.

If you're unsure on where or how to start, treat yourself like you would treat your newborn baby. Nourish your body, bathe, take yourself on a walk, read a book to yourself, get some face time with your loved ones, and get back to basics. Eventually, you will feel yourself on stabler ground with that chalk-board of habits, and you'll start to take more notice of the empty one. Write these down on it: speaking kindly to yourself, noticing which habits from the "here and now" board feel forced and which come easily, finding new ways to practice the ones that come easily to you, learning to meditate and actually sticking with it, holding space for yourself and your feelings (FEEL your feelings), and figuring out and practicing what valuing yourself over others really looks like.

Currently, my self-care is catching and reframing negative thoughts about my postpartum body, healing my relationship with food and exercise, med-itating every day (something I've wanted to do for years), knowing that it is more than ok to want more than motherhood, and endless self-develop-ment. Now, this next part is very important, perhaps the MOST important part: Self-care and self-development are not one-size-fits-all. I know you don't want to hear this, but there is not just one book, one podcast, one course, one routine, or one person who can tell you what to do and how to do it in order to heal and become the best version of yourself. But what you can do is take a little something from each book, podcast, course, routine, and person to *slowly and over time* build your own path. Trust me when I say that I did not want this to be true. It's tedious and rigorous work, but you know as well I do that the only way we heal and grow is by turning inward to the core of who we are. We have all that we need inside of us; we just need help uncovering it.

So I just threw a bunch of self-helpy words at you, words you've heard one thousand times before and words that pained me to read while deep in the throes of depression. But remember this: If I, Christie Rocha, now 3 and ½ years beyond the lowest, darkest moments of my life, when I wanted noth-ing to do with this stuff, can write and offer these words to you, they must be true. I am your evidence.

I am a Mother. I started this chapter by sharing a painful confession, and I'm going to end it with a startling one, as I'm having this realization in real time. So that means you are the first to hear this: I ultimately went from depressed and immobile to writing this chapter because I am a mother. Yup. Ok, I'm tearing up now. I've had a beef with motherhood since I became a mother. I hated breastfeeding, sleep deprivation is something I wouldn't wish on my worst enemy, I missed spontaneous date nights with my husband, and friends drifted. Everything about motherhood seemed to test me and what I thought of myself, my self-esteem, my worth, my passions, my desires, my abilities, everything. I felt like I was failing a test I thought I'd ace. At my lowest point, I knew there was a miniscule part of me somewhere really deep down and far away that I knew I had to wake up. And I knew that I wanted to live to see another day. I never thought about ending my life, but I got to a point where I could understand how people did.

But those kids, those sweet faces, tiny hands, tiny feet, and tiny toes are truly what kept me going. They are what kept me sure that I wanted more from a "happy place" than lying down in darkness. The beautiful thing about this is that now that I'm on the other side. I truly keep growing and healing for myself.

Remember this: When we do for ourselves, we do for our kids. My growth and empowerment is their growth and empowerment. I am your evidence.

Chapter 7
ELISHA ZAVIER
www.vlounge.ca | @mamapreneur.vs.adhd

Prelude to a Storm

I was diagnosed with ADD as a kid in the '90s where neurodiversity was celebrated with medication, labels, aaannnndddd stigmaaasss! There wasn't a whole lot of great information, research, tools, or resources out there (certainly not to the level we have now!), so my parents did what most parents at the time did: they followed the advice of the medical professionals they were referred to. And back then, doctors were handing out Ritalin prescriptions like a freakin' PEZ dispenser.

I did not like being medicated. I wasn't me. I was withdrawn and quiet. It felt like I was a shell of myself. So eventually, I went off them and tried to fend for myself. I learned how to manage my symptoms by using organizers, different coloured pens, highlighters, music to drown out the noise, and a solid routine. None of these things stopped me from living in a world of forgetfulness, procrastination, and last-minute hyperfocus. I thrived in the drama and excitement of a time crunch.

The label of ADD slowly disappeared. As I got older, it didn't seem to factor into anything I did. I didn't even think about it anymore as it related to how I operated day to day. I mean, sure I was easily excitable (I call it very passionate) and distra—SQUIRRREELLL!! And I still sometimes leave things to the last minute, but everyone does that, right?

My point is that I'd spent the majority of my adult life thinking I didn't have ADD anymore, at least not in the context of what we now understand and know about it. I had the time, space, and ability to process my emotions, compartmentalize, and deal with whatever I was facing. And I spent YEARS in therapy getting over generational trauma so that it wouldn't factor into my parenting. I vowed to do better. (That's a very separate story, but I love my parents for giving me the ability to think for myself and take ownership for my actions regardless of how they parented me; it wasn't perfect, and they did the best with what was available to them at the time. They also taught me that when you know better, you can do better!)

The reality was that my symptoms were alive and well; I just didn't associate them with ADD. I mean, how many coffee tumblers do I have to forget on shelves at Winners to connect the dots that it hadn't really gone away?

And Now Back to Our Regularly Scheduled Mama Journey Programming...

I spent years dreaming of having a baby. I started a list of names when I was, like, twelve. But my son was not given a name from that list because they were all girls' names! When my partner and I decided it was time, we got pregnant right away (I'm a fertile myrtle. It's a curse and blessing, but that's also a story for another time). I was very lucky, and I had an amazing pregnancy. In fact, I loved being pregnant. I felt strong and powerful and sexy as hell. I remember thinking "I'm going to love having a baby." (Notice how I didn't say I was going to be a mom? It didn't occur to me, at the time, that they were different).

I was going to have a natural childbirth, exclusively breastfeed, make homemade purees, do everything organic, and make ALL the crafts. My baby was going to read, and I was going to have the most amazing relationship with my child. I was going to be "that mom."

I was in for a rather blunt awakening.

I talked about my birthing wishes with my partner, how it was important for me not to be medicated, and that an epidural was a last resort. We talked about ways he could help me—massage, breathing, walking, and we even made a labour playlist with my favourite power anthems to keep me focused (DMX, Salt-N-Pepa, and Ludacris were on that playlist, just so you have an idea of where my headspace was at). I sent him Pinterest images of the pictures I wanted to capture, so we can have these beautifully staged memories.

We were educated about PPD during our birthing class, and we were handed a bunch of pamphlets so he could "watch for the signs" after I delivered our son. Postpartum mental health is way more in the forefront of medical conversation and mainstream media now than it was even 10 years ago. But still, neither of us were adequately prepared for the shitshow that ensued.

I feel like I wanted to stay cocooned in my happy little place of what my expectations were about motherhood, and I wasn't attuned to other messages about some of the realities. Plus, NO ONE in my circle with kids really painted an accurate picture. Everyone seemed more concerned about my physical pregnancy—how amazing I looked, how beautiful growing life was, how much I was going to love it, and they asked if I was nesting and what my birth plan was. The pregnancy pages and social media I was following seemed to be targeting me with hyper-focused information on pregnancy, so I spent 9 months being bombarded with specific baby and pregnancy info like how to manage nausea, why there's hair there, not to be surprised that I was going poop while labouring (this one was indeed a surprise), choosing nursery colours, and picking out baby names. You know, the super useful content bites. I was, like, "I'm going to be fine... This is going to be amazing. Sure my life will change, but it's gonna be a AH-fucking-MAZING."

Ready or not, here he comes! I won't go into the full details of my birth experience, just the extended highlight reel. I ended up being induced at almost 42 weeks, even though I didn't want to be; it was necessary, apparently. I didn't get to have that labour at home and anxiously time the contractions experience or have my water break in the middle of a store or outing. A doctor broke my water with a stick.

I was promptly given Pitocin, which I understood was going to bring on contractions. But what I didn't realize was that you (me, specifically) would go from ZERO to HOLY MOTHER OF EFFING GOD in a matter of minutes!! There was no gradual build up, and no getting into a rhythm. Almost immediately, I experienced blinding contractions that made me want to pass out. And I very quickly gave up. "Babe, I want the drugs!!" I didn't have a doula or midwife in my corner to fight for my birthing wishes; I had a husband who saw how in pain and scared I suddenly looked, and he just wanted to make it better. He was just as scared and nervous as I was and didn't know what else to do.

Once the epidural and fentanyl were administered, I was NOT present, and my husband sat on his phone while I drifted in and out of consciousness, unable to express how much I NEEDED him to be present for me. After the initial drug wave wore off, I became fully aware that my dreams of walking around, kneeling, bending, bouncing on a ball, and labouring out of a bed were not going to happen.

The rest of my labour continued with my husband sitting on his phone and me laying in bed, uncomfortably experiencing waves of tolerable pain because the epidural only worked on half my body! We sat in silence, for the most part, with the occasional "you ok?," popsicle trip, and progress checks from the nurses. He didn't really show up until it was pushing time. I didn't realize it then, but being abandoned and deprived of the birthing experience I imagined would end up being the catalyst for my feelings of disappointment surrounding my motherhood journey.

When my son was finally out, and they put him on me for the first time, I didn't really feel a thing! Maybe it was the drugs, the 12 hours labouring without support, or the 2 hours of pushing, but that euphoria of new mom love was not there. Cherubs weren't flying around our room, and the orchestra wasn't playing; there was just nothing.

What was wrong with me? That would not be the last time I would ask myself that question.

We had some trouble with latching at first, and I was told by the lactation specialist that I had shitty (my word) inverted nipples, and she promptly gave me a plastic syringe tube to plump them up (I'm laughing now, but that was a crushing blow less than 24 hours after delivering my son). She wasn't supportive or encouraging. I was just another patient she had to see on the floor that day, and I was quickly left to figure it out on my own. Eventually we got latched—or so I thought—and off we continued. I remember how relieved and proud I felt when that moment happened. I snapped a pic and sent it to my hubby; I got an "attaboy" style response. The lactation specialist never came back, and we were sent home.

Two or three days later, at our very first paediatric follow up, I was told our son wasn't "thriving"—low milk supply, apparently. But I was determined to give my son every ounce of that liquid gold I could get in him. And again, that question crept up... What was wrong with me? I had ONE function as his mom, as a woman: to nourish and feed my baby. And I couldn't even get that right. What was wrong with me?

(On a side note, telling a new mom that her baby isn't thriving and placing the blame on her is a really bad practice. These feelings of shame and guilt are fed to us by supposed "medical professionals" and then supercharged by our already vulnerable mental state.)

After a week of having him on my boobs ALL the time and pumping in between to increase my milk supply, my child still wasn't getting the nutrients he needed. We HAD to supplement with formula. The decision sent me into a spiral of self-loathing, disappointment, and guilt. I had dreamed of breastfeeding exclusively, and in that moment, my dream was completely shattered. I researched for hours and hours about the best formula, all the while cringing at the ingredient lists and chemicals and risks. I was feeling more guilt over making sure I was picking the right one. Finally, I found one that I was comfortable with that was in Europe, and so we had it shipped by the case load.

For five and a half months, I juggled breastfeeding, pumping, and preparing bottles. I was on medication to keep what little supply I had (a medication that, with my blood disorder, could have killed me if I wasn't careful), and I ate lactation cookies by the container full, thanks to my amazing mom who baked them for me! While things were simpler when I stopped breastfeeding, I never really got to fully compartmentalize or deal with any of those emotions and the fact that I felt like a failure. I just had to keep going.

At some point, we had friends. And one time while we were getting food set up for some guests we had over, my son started wailing. He was hungry, and we needed to prep a bottle for him. I was frantically trying to soothe him and get the bottle warmed up when my friend's husband yelled "Put that baby on a tit already!" As if I wasn't already desperately trying to make the crying stop, I needed a reminder from another person (an asshole, at that) of just how inadequate I was. I carried that comment with me for a long time.

A Peek Inside my Overactive Brain

Why is going anywhere so difficult and draining? Did I pack everything? Do I have enough extra clothes, diapers, wipes, creams, lotions, formula, breast pump, bottles, nipple shield, toys—oh, and don't forget the baby!

Why won't he sleep? Why does he wake up the second I put him in his bassinet? Why does he wake up before he's supposed to? All the articles I'm reading keep saying he needs to sleep more for his brain development. Why can he only fall asleep on me? I know I should savour these snuggles, but all I can think about is how badly I want just a little space and a freakin' shower. What's wrong with me? Why don't I love this? Am I a bad mom? It's been 4 months of having a baby sleep on me all day. Do I smell funny? (I have been told that I was definitely smelly!)

Am I making the right decisions? Is he warm enough, cool enough, and fed enough? Is he tired, hungry, or uncomfortable, or does he just have to fart? Should I have listened to my mom when she told me NOT to get him used to sleeping in a completely dark room with a sound machine? 'Cause now I can't go anywhere. I'm tied to my house for naps. I can't go out ANYWHERE. I don't see my friends anymore. Why isn't anyone coming to visit us? I miss my old life. I was so free. Why don't I love this yet? I just want to scream. Why do I feel so angry?

Why did I ever think I could do this (have a baby)? I suck at it. I hate so many parts of it. Does everyone feel like this? Why would anyone want to feel like this? Why did I want to have a baby so badly? This was a mistake. They don't deserve this. They'd be better off without me. But I can't leave...

Manifesting Rage

I remember the first time I raged in front of my son. He was 6-ish months old. And to be honest, I don't think I have ever told anyone about this. I'm so ashamed that I've kept it to myself in fear that it was just more proof of how utterly horrific and undeserving I was as a mother. I was in our bathroom trying to get him down for his nap, with the fan on, in complete darkness, holding him a very specific way, shushing in a patterned tone, and bouncing with a specific motion—while he wailed in my ear. With no sign of him settling, I started feeling this heat rise up from my chest; an uncontrollable volcanic eruption was brewing, and my insides were trembling. After 30 minutes of this, I grabbed his little calf, squeezed it, and screamed "WHY WON'T YOU JUST GO TO SLEEP?!" Immediately, I placed him in the middle of my bed and walked away, bawling uncontrollably.

WHAT'S WRONG WITH ME!?!? I talked with a trusted mental health professional about how I felt (not all the particulars), who assured me that moments like those were, in fact, normal, and that what I had experienced was something she, too, went through. Our conversation surrounding this "feeling" is a little blurry now, but the gist was that if I felt that way again, I should give the baby to my husband/parents/in-laws/any other human being close

71

by or put him down somewhere safe and go have a cry or yell in private. IN PRIVATE. Let it out and carry on.

I continued managing that rage with a lot of exhausting energy that seemingly only masked its existence, all the while I thought things were getting better. I was distracted because we were moving, but the invisible load of motherhood continued its exponential expansion with the entire world of my baby resting solely on my shoulders. I kept the façade going, even to myself.

But deep inside, my resentment and anger silently grew with every disappointment: no one acknowledging my first Mother's Day the way I had hoped, our families who had other life priorities, my friends without kids not getting it, and my partner who didn't take pictures of our son sleeping on my chest (or any, for that matter). Every moment where I sacrificed myself, where I neglected my self-care, or where my actions went unnoticed and underappreciated just added to the pile of my feeling unworthy. It wasn't evident to me at the time just how much I was internalizing these things, but there were noticeable shifts in my behaviour and mental health that started surfacing following the next series of events.

Just before my son turned 1, and my mat leave was coming to an end, I had to start thinking about what me working would look like for our family. My job was in the city, which meant an almost 3-hour commute on top of my 8-hour work day. We weren't quite ready for full-time childcare. My son needed to sleep a specific way, and daycare wasn't conducive to that (AKA my anxiety about his sleep needs prevented my brain from letting go). Plus, I didn't like the idea of missing his entire day. So I decided to become my own boss! I kept my position with my employer, but I started billing for my time instead of being paid a salary, with the understanding that I would be starting with reduced hours and spending 1 day a week in the office. I had time to work when my son napped and in the evenings when he was sleeping. I felt I could make it work, basing this on my level of production, efficiency, and focus from how I USED to work.

It was supposed to mean flexibility, but what it turned into was the full-blown activation of my underlying... (yet to be named).

The Shitstorm Begins...

When I started working again, I immediately began to subconsciously shift my priorities. The pressure of meeting deadlines and being accountable while simultaneously having to care for an unpredictable tiny human made me feel anxious, overwhelmed, even more inadequate, and angry. The very things that made my beautiful child who he was were the things that often caused me to feel shitty about being behind at work. All these feelings created an incredibly toxic home environment that I soon lost control of.

What's wrong with me? Why can't I do anything like how I used to?

It didn't help that I ended up being the default parent. If you're not familiar with that term, it means I was responsible for EVERYTHING as it pertained to our child. I was the key master and keeper of all the things. I filled in paperwork, booked appointments, tracked growth and feeding amounts, and cooked all his food. If he was sick, I had to shuffle around my entire life to stay with him. I was constantly being asked questions about what was going on, where things were, and how to do things for him.

Most mornings, I woke up wondering if it was all a nightmare. Then I'd hear "Mama," and those feelings would come rushing back. Pervasive negative thoughts, emotions, memories, disappointment, and unfulfilled expectations all washed over me at the same time, living rent free in every nook and cranny of my inner dialogue.

Why couldn't I just have a "normal" motherhood experience? Having a baby was a mistake. I'll just pack the necessities and leave everything else behind. I'll get a job somewhere and just keep putting money into an account for them. They'll be better off if I'm not here to ruin everything. But I have nowhere to go, and my son will keep asking for me. He'll forget me, though... And they deserve better than me. I ruin everything that's good. What's wrong with me?

There is literally nothing that's gone right or as expected or anywhere close to what I wanted or imagined. And for a long time, I struggled with accepting that THIS was the experience I would remember, instead of the one I had envisioned. It made me long for something that was never going to be. I was sad, angry, and disappointed, and I was getting tired of feeling that way.

It's a very strange feeling to love something so fiercely but also resent and hate parts of it just as fiercely. I love my son with every ounce of my being, but I also battled with SOMETHING for most of my motherhood journey, and I had no idea how to name it.

I asked myself, "What's wrong with me?" more times than I can count in the first 4 years of being a mother. I've been asked, "What's wrong with you?" by my husband and told that family members were asking him, "What's wrong with her?" I had been told that "a mother shouldn't feel or behave like this," without a single person offering to help or provide support. Maybe they did in the only way they knew how, and I didn't see it because they didn't know how to reach me.

I feel like I was chronically in survival mode, with flight or fight mode always on.

And I was not OK. Far from it, and I had no idea why or how to fix it. I had no name or label for it, and I was chasing an explanation, a cause, a reason, or something to blame other than to conclude that I was irreversibly broken. I wanted to break a cycle I was responsible for creating without any tools to figure it out and too much shame to ask for help. What I found were acronyms on Google, on Facebook, and in books as well as some that were provided by my medical professionals that I could use to explain or treat it: PPD, PPA, OCD, CBT, and ACT (Postpartum Depression/Anxiety, Obsessive Compulsive Disorder, Cognitive Behavior Therapy, and Acceptance & Commitment Therapy).

The help I did seek probably wasn't the right kind of help. With long wait times for provincial access, costly hourly visits (health benefits only go so far), and my lack of prioritizing myself, I continued to fall through the cracks of a system that didn't prioritize mothers' mental health and ultimately failed by misunderstanding my symptoms and self-imposed isolation.

When I finally did manage to get an appointment with a psychotherapist, I had a 30-minute consult, where I described what I was feeling as persistent negative thoughts that would keep popping into my brain on repeat. (I always offer full transparency of my symptoms and history to every medical professional; I'm an open book.) The doctor responded with "Oh, ok. Sounds like a type of OCD. I'll prescribe an antipsychotic at a low dose to start."

I'm no mental health professional, so I agreed to try. At this point, I just wanted it to stop. Suffice it to say, it didn't work. I had booked a follow-up appointment that I inevitably had to reschedule, and the next appointment was, like, 2 months away. And by that time, I'd run out of the meds and was worse off than when I'd started.

I was at my wits' end, well over a year later, when I had another go at therapy. This doctor thought I needed to work ACT (Acceptance & Commitment Therapy—a practice of learning how to control thought using visualizations or other mindfulness techniques) into my life. While he validated a little of what I was feeling, there wasn't a diagnosis, and the words PPD were never spoken. This didn't end up working for me for a couple of reasons: timing (I ended up breaking my foot and not being able to drive), and I wasn't mentally ready to take on this new practice. Now, I know what you're thinking: "You keep saying you wanted it to end." Yes, I did. And I have no explanation for why I felt this wasn't the thing that was going to fix me; it just wasn't. Maybe I just wanted a proper assessment and a clinical diagnosis, so I could find a cookie-cutter solution that would just make it magically disappear. But it didn't exist, and I needed to put in the work. I just didn't know it then. Nor did I have the bandwidth to add yet another thing onto my evergrowing to-do list that I could barely get through or keep up with in the first place.

The one positive thing that came out of my sessions with this treatment was a visualization tool I use to help with my negative self-talk. The exercise is to take a negative thought, acknowledge it by putting it on a leaf, and then watch it float away. There's a little more to it, but you get the idea.

Ok, so I'm not delicate, politically correct, or granola enough that that was going to work for me. I needed something that was more fitting to how I handle my problems—a little more sparkly!

I'm Not a Control Freak—You Are!

I've definitely been told that I have some control issues (Uumm, helllooo ADHD and perfectionism). It's something I've learned really hard to TRY and give up as a parent, but that's still a work in progress.

In April of 2019, I broke my right foot, and suddenly I needed help—a lot of help. And, you guessed it: asking for and receiving help are not my strong suits. Someone had to be with me at all times whenever my son was around. He wasn't quite 3 yet, he required a decent amount of attention and engagement, he was not potty trained, and I had a lot of mobility/balance issues, with my foot being non-weight bearing.

This is where things started REALLY taking a turn for the worse. I was completely not in control of what was happening in my environment. I had my parents or in-laws around ALL the time. I was crawling out of my own skin. It was pure chaos. Everything got out of whack—all of our routines and systems. If you know me, you'll know that I don't do well with people in my space for prolonged periods of time. I felt so unheard that I literally screamed at the top of my lungs—at everyone.

I continued reliving each disappointment, unmet need, and unrealistic expectation that came up every day to the point of demolishing my confidence, my happiness, my gratitude, and my self-worth. It made me question everything I did, every choice I'd made, and every unknown encounter. Everything I lost control over became enraging to me.

The effects of this lasted for months, even after my foot had healed. I became short-tempered, impatient, aggressive, and mean. I raged with increasing brutality, in unfiltered, emotionally unregulated tantrums that left my husband walking on eggshells and my son scared of his mama (he actually called me a monster, more than once, and it was heartbreaking). This continued to amplify, and all my insecurities manifested as unchecked rage and a complete disregard for myself and my self-care. I experienced weight gain, regular anxiety and panic attacks, and a self-hatred I've never experienced before.

There were (and still are) days that I didn't want to be a mom anymore, when my child danced on my every nerve (it almost seemed intentional, even though I know better). There were days that my then threenager was so infuriating that I wanted to (and did) punch walls and slam doors. Truth be told, I had thoughts of punching him on more than one occasion, where the rage I felt inside was almost blinding, and a powerful cascade of triggering emotions followed. I often hid behind pleasantries and told people I was just having a rough day. The idea of having to verbalize my true thoughts and feelings was paralyzing.

On a daily basis, I had to convince myself not to leave, feeling completely trapped by a choice that I had made. I told myself that I was completely unequipped to do this and that I have no idea what I'm doing, as a mother and sometimes even as an adult. I was left wondering why I kept feeling this way and desperately wanting and trying, through tears and shame, not to feel this way anymore.

How I started healing was by being more engaged, honest, and authentic in a private mom community I was a part of (I know the founder, and she hates the idea of a mom group, but this was so much more than that—we were queens) and participating in a few maternal mental health events. Over the years, I've shared versions of this story and updates on treatments and self/medical interventions and how I was feeling. Someone replied to me once and said something that really hit home. I had posted about the negative self-talk I was experiencing and she replied with:

"Would you ever let your friends talk to you like that?" And I thought to myself, "FUCK, NO. I wouldn't even let a stranger talk to me that way. I'd kick their ass or verbally assault them."

The battle was how to attack those negative thoughts when they crept in. This is where that ACT visualization clicked. I started picturing a little ninja karate kicking/chopping/punching/roundhousing them away whilst saying "HI-YAH!" Changing the internal conversation I was having in my head required work, and it required me actually doing the work. But it was worth it.

Just for Fun, Let's Throw a Pandemic into the Mix and See What She Does.

They whispered to her, "You can't withstand the storm." She whispered back, "I AM THE STORM."

COVID-19 ended up being the best thing that happened to us. But it got a little worse before it got better. Thrown into spending every waking hour with each other, the adults in the room struggled to keep it together—me, especially. Now I had to work from home with my toddler. We had no idea WTF was going on, but everything changed instantly. I'm not going to go too deep into this because WE ALL know what happened, and it affected every. single. person. differently.

On May 5, 2020, I wrote:

Today I feel like a complete failure. I failed as a mother, profoundly. I yelled at my kid; it was not the first time. It was not the first time I felt like a failure. I squashed a little piece of my child's spark today, and I don't know how to fix it. I feel frustrated, sad, ashamed, and disgusted with myself. My husband and I fought in front of our son; it was not the first time he's heard us speak badly of each other. Today, my husband reminded me again that I am supposed to be the role model for good behaviour, but I, too, am acting like a toddler. I feel lost. Why can't I reign it in? What is triggering it, and why can't I stop it from erupting?

After several learning curves, outbursts, tantrums (adults included), and some very dark places, we got into a rhythm. But in order for that to happen, I NEEDED to make a change. I NEEDED an answer, and suddenly no one in the world was available to talk to me. I started reading, exploring, and listening to those external messages about motherhood and about all the forces contributing to how I felt. I found a medical professional on Instagram who actually saw the bigger picture of what I was experiencing and, for the first time, conceptualized it: Postpartum Rage. She spoke a mama acknowledgement language that I was so attuned to and ready to receive. She also happened to be local, which was just a little icing on the cake. I love supporting the community I live in.

Did you even know Postpartum Rage was a real thing? I sure didn't. Finally, an answer, an explanation, some reason for the crazy rhyme, and finally some VALIDATION. After spending years hiding and feeling unworthy, I could identify what I was feeling.

"Anger is sometimes overlooked when diagnosing a woman with a postpartum mood disorder. One 2018 study from the University of British Columbia noted that women need to be screened specifically for anger, which hasn't been done in the past."[1]*

I started doing more of the work: reading, watching, and participating. I did a workshop and got some tools that I started using immediately. Managing my emotions and trying to change a vicious cycle with a toddler took a lot of time and energy!

Work Work Work Work Work

Watching my child discover, explore, and navigate through this world is joyous. The sheer happiness he experiences when he sees something new or figures something out is incredible. But teaching him boundaries, natural consequences, and rules was incredibly deflating.

Some of the best advice and tools I got was from social media. Instagram ended up being a source for some amazing resources that I implemented to improve how I communicate and start to repair the relationships with my son, my partner, and myself. The situations they described with easy-

1   Frost, Alexandra. "Postpartum Rage: The Unspoken Emotion of New Motherhood." *Healthline*, 29 Apr. 2020, www.healthline.com/health/postpartum-rage. Accessed 2 May 2023.

Christine H. Ou, Wendy A. Hall. Anger in the context of postnatal depression: An integrative review. Birth, 2018; DOI: 10.1111/birt.12356

to-follow instructions to resolve the problem, language and explanations to use (verbatim!), fun reels, and totally relatable solutions helped me.

I signed up to work with a nutrition and mindset coach to build better habits. We used daily affirmations, to-do lists, mental reprogramming of my internal voice, and ways to make new routines stick—with accountability. I had to prioritize myself again and bring back some very basic needs that I had neglected for too long: quality sleep, movement I love, eating habits to fuel my body, and things that make me happy. But it was the check-ins and the 1:1 support that made this stick. The best part was that she was also a mom and could relate to what I was going through.

I started feeling connected again. Even as I write this, I can hardly believe my behaviour and am in complete AWE that my wonderful, resilient child is still incredibly happy and has come out of this mostly unscathed. I commend my husband for being an incredible father. He may, at times, be a completely emotionally unaware human being (which is also work we're doing together), but he is truly an amazing partner. Our relationship is the best it's ever been, which not only did we need for us, but more so we needed it for our son.

Here's my list of favourite mom IG accounts:

- @momwell (This is who I did my rage workshop with.)
- @goodnessinsideout (This is the coach I used and now work with 'cause she's so good!)
- @psychedmommy
- @transformingtoddlerhood
- @dr.siggie (She's one of the best, in my opinion, with some amazing freebies!)
- @mamapsychologists
- @biglittlefeelings (This is my other favourite; just amazing.)
- @mommacusses (Gwen explains gentle parenting in a way my inner rebel jives with so much.)

ADHD'er for Life

A male coworker of mine used to say that a woman loses parts of her brain with every pregnancy/child. I used to laugh with him about it, but now I have a very different perspective. Moms spend a great deal of time and energy making thousands of decisions for a whole other being, so it's not that we lose part of our brains; it's that ALL our resources are reallocated.

While I got much better at managing the energy and tone of the communication in our house—and I was feeling better about myself—there was still something off. I was still overwhelmed, overstimulated, and anxious, and the same heat would build in my chest when I was triggered. This is where I started noticing how my work still continued to impact me, but the other part of that was HOW I was working. It felt very discombobulated. I was constantly getting distracted, getting interrupted, and not staying organized. I felt like I could never finish anything; switching tasks became increasingly more difficult, everything took forever to do, and I was always behind.

According to the CADDAC (Centre for ADHD Awareness, Canada) attention-deficit/hyperactivity disorder (ADHD) affects approximately 1.8 million Canadians (4-6% of adults and 5-7% of children) – that's 1 in every about 21 people[2]. I have ADHD, and I had always suspected that my son had ADHD, too. And then I saw in him some of those characteristics that were associated with the ADD I understood from so long ago. I knew that if I was going to help him, I had to learn more and start working on verbalizing my ADHD needs. And I needed to teach him tools that would be successful for him.

Twenty-seven years after my initial diagnosis, we now understand ADHD very differently. Firstly, ADD is an outdated diagnosis that isn't even used anymore. ADHD stands for attention-deficit/hyperactivity disorder. There are 2 key elements: inattentive and hyperactive/impulsive. ADHD as we know it today has transformed: from ADD with/without hyperactivity to ADHD without subtypes and now updated to 3 subtypes of ADHD: inattentive, hyperactive/impulsive, and combined type.

2   "About ADHD." *Centre for ADHD Awareness, Canada*, caddac.ca/about-adhd/. Accessed 2 May 2023.

Secondly, females exhibit symptoms of ADHD very differently, but we live in a world where research money is focused on boys/men and then applied to girls/women—cause we're the same, right?! (dripping in sarcasm)

Most importantly, we understand that it is indeed a specific neurodevelopmental disorder (there were mixed reviews on what it was, with some claiming it was a behavioural issue), which means there's brain science to explain what's happening. The behaviours behind those labels of troublemaker, lazy, rude, or not listening are actually rooted in how the brain produces and delivers specific neurotransmitters. The deficiencies play a role in 4 key areas of brain functionality for people with ADHD: executive functioning, emotional regulation, attentiveness, and hyperactivity.

And! It's very common for changes and fluctuations in hormones (AAAHH-HEEEEMMMM pregnancy!!) or big life changes/stressors (AAAHHHEEEEM-MMM having a baby, not grieving my old life, work pressure, adulting, a fucking pandemic, and owning my own business) to trigger or worsen symptoms.

Looking back at my "symptoms" and learning about my own ADHD, I can see how it went completely unnoticed, unchecked, and disregarded for so long.

I once again turned to social media and found a plethora (I love that word!) of amazing accounts that have helped me so much! This is still a relatively new development, and I continue to be a work in progress with it. But I am hopeful...

If you had told me 5 years ago that I would feel this good now, I probably wouldn't have believed you. I love where I am, and I love that I've DONE THE WORK to get here.

So now, through teaching my child how to love his unique way of thinking, I am teaching myself, too. We don't talk about ADHD as a diagnosis for either of us; my son doesn't even know he has it. We learn ways to adapt, problem solve, and build healthy habits to help him thrive—together. On a side note, that doesn't always happen, and sometimes I just need to do things my way, which often means me taking more time—case in point: this book! I missed my deadline, but I'm so proud of what I did here.

Here's my list of favourite ADHD IG accounts:

- · @myladyadhd
- · @adhdbrainhealth
- · @thepsychdoctormd
- · @adhd_love_
- · @future.adhd
- · @adhddoers
- · @drbrianftw

Happily Ever After

I don't know when it happened, but somewhere through the murk and the mud, I fell in love with my son, unconditionally. And now every day, my goal is to build his spark up. Our relationship is not perfect, but we communicate with each other a lot better. I model by apologizing and showing my son that I am nothing if not a HUMAN BEING trying to do better.

When I thought about entering motherhood, did I ever expect to feel ANY of this?! NO. Did I want to feel this way?! FUCK, NO. Can I change it? Every damn day, I do my best to do better and keep trying. I will also keep forgiving myself, giving myself grace, and working towards improving.

A Letter to the Old Me

You are so full of gumption and grit and sass, and you're so sure of who you are with unwavering resolve and passion. It's OK if you get a little lost along the way. Your values, beliefs, and character are still at your core. It's OK if things don't work out the exact way you envisioned. You can make a new path that's just as beautiful. You are capable beyond your perceived weaknesses. Embrace the lessons, lean on people's strengths, and grow together. You are so much more than your doubts and your fears. Take the risks; the rewards are worth it. You—just you—are enough.

That girl is still in there.

Chapter 8
JESSICA SAWYER
@jsawyer240

Hello, eating disorder—a disease that robs you of your joy, makes you question everything about your body, tricks you into thinking that you aren't good enough, and is all consuming. To begin my journey to motherhood, we need to go back about 15 years to when I was a teen. An eating disorder consumed many of my young teenage years, a time in a young woman's life when she is so vulnerable to the influences of that "perfect body image" that was such a strong focus of many magazines and television shows of the early 2000s. We weren't yet big into social media, but television and magazines still had a huge influence.

Some of my goals as a young teen were to lose "X" number of pounds, because then so-and-so may notice me and like me. I was a bookworm blessed with braces and glasses, and I was constantly being bullied. Oh, and did I mention that my mom worked at the same school I attended? I was so "not cool." I felt like an outsider during much of my time in public school, and the eating disorder was something that I could actually control. I would restrict my meals or how much I ate at a meal, and then I would sneak downstairs to our basement and run on our elliptical to see if I could quickly burn some calories, so I could feel better about eating "too much." This went on until I was hospitalized at 15 due to heart concerns from low blood pressure and pulse. The doctors were worried that my heart wouldn't be able to support my bodily functions. For two months, I was force-fed; I never had a G-tube, but meals were supervised and if I didn't eat within a certain time limit, I would have to have a supplement shake. When I hit an acceptable weight, I was finally sent home, but I had spent my 16th birthday celebrating in a hospital room with only my family.

Just because I was discharged at an acceptable weight, that doesn't mean that I was cured from having an eating disorder. In my opinion, I don't think you can ever be "cured" in the sense that we view that word. You still have disordered thoughts about yourself and your body image, and you will sometimes still have trouble accepting food as fuel. There will always be a little voice in the back of your head questioning you and sometimes judging you. You need to do a lot of mental work to ignore that voice and to learn to love your body for the amazing things that it can do on a daily basis. I don't own a scale in my house, and that is one way I cope. I don't want to know my weight, and that is one way I ensure I don't focus on the restricting patterns I had in the past.

When dealing with my eating disorder, I was always told that I needed to ensure I gained weight because otherwise, I might never be able to have kids in the future (I did lose my period for six months while I was going through everything). In certain cases, I am sure that there is truth in that statement. So when I finally came off birth control in 2019, I was so shocked and excited that I was able to get pregnant on my third month off medication. I thought it was an absolute miracle! I had battled disordered eating thoughts for years, and was miraculously able to come right off birth control and get pregnant right away. What wonderful news!

Seeing those lines on the pregnancy test was when it actually hit me how much I wanted to become a mother. I could feel it so deeply within my heart that this was what I wanted more than anything. Before this moment, I had thought that if I get pregnant, then I do; If I don't, then that's okay, and I will deal with it. But that positive line on the test changed my whole view. I was so excited, and I could not wait for this baby to arrive. The date was December 27th, 2019.

Now I had to come up with a creative way to tell my husband. Do I create a surprise cake? Wrap presents with clues? Give him a fun shirt? I spent hours searching Pinterest for the perfect way to surprise him. I am terrible at keeping secrets, especially if I have to surprise someone. I quickly went to Walmart and found a cute onesie that said "Hello World," had a friend knit a pair of booties, and grabbed a few other baby-related items. I was able to contain this news until New Year's Eve, and then surprised my husband with the gift. I'd never seen him so excited, once he finally figured out what the gift meant for us.

Cue the phone calls to both sets of parents. We decided to let them know right away, as they were all going to be grandparents for the first time with the arrival of this baby. We didn't think anything else of it; why would we? We were on cloud nine. This news was quickly followed by a doctor's appointment to review everything and to check blood work to confirm that everything was okay. It was! The doctor gave me an overview of what to do and what not to do and booked the next appointment. That's when the news really set in: We were really going to have a baby!

Now I had to keep it from my co-workers. I owned a pharmacy at this time and was always working. I'm a workaholic, working over 12 hours a day, and I knew that my staff would catch on quickly—and they did. By the end of the week, one of my employees saw me sitting down for longer than five minutes (I never sit down!), looking sick. They jokingly asked, "What, are you pregnant?" The look on my face gave me away immediately, and the secret was out.

A few days later, I woke up feeling super tired, so I decided to take a morning nap and planned to head into work later that afternoon. I woke up from my nap with a bit of spotting, but I just told myself it wasn't much and was probably normal. I had to get to work and host a meeting, so I just put it at the back of my mind. By the time the meeting was over, it was more than spotting, but I didn't know what to do. I was still thinking that this was probably normal. Should I keep working? That was my plan. Or should I bother the doctors at emerg for something that could be normal? My staff finally convinced me that this was not normal, and that I needed to be seen by a doctor. This began the longest few days of waiting...

In emerg, they called in the ultrasound technician to do an ultrasound, and they completed blood work. Without a baseline blood work panel, they wouldn't be able to tell if my HCG hormones had increased like they should, or if they had decreased. I had to wait another 48 hours to complete another round of blood work to determine if the bleeding was normal or if it was indicative of a miscarriage. The ultrasound also wasn't very helpful. I was only 6.5 weeks along, and they couldn't find a heartbeat. This was quite common early in pregnancy. All they could say was, "Go home, sleep, rest, and wait until the next set of blood work is done in 48 hours."

I remember going home feeling absolutely devastated. How could this happen? What were the test results going to say? Over the next two days, I still kept bleeding, but I was holding onto a small sliver of hope that this was normal and that I was not having a miscarriage. Unfortunately, the 48-hour blood work fell on a Friday, so I knew I would be going into the weekend still not knowing the answer. The doctor who I had seen earlier in the week was working in emerg over the weekend, and on Saturday, I got the dreaded news: my HCG levels had dropped, and I was bleeding because I was having a miscarriage.

After actually hearing it vocalized, I was even more devastated by the news. Deep down, I had known days prior that I was having a miscarriage; I could feel the changes in my body. The guilt you experience after having a miscarriage is huge, even though there is nothing you could have done to prevent it. I would ask myself, "Was it because of that drink I had the night before I found out I was pregnant? Is work too stressful? Did I lift something too heavy? Was it because of my history with an eating disorder, and my body just hated me?" These types of questions would run through my mind on a daily basis and lay a huge guilt trip on me.

I had my miscarriage in January of 2020, and two months later, the world shut down. I was not finished my grieving, and grieving when all you can do is go to work and come home is HARD. I'm not going to lie. Grieving is also hard when everyone in the world has no idea what's going on and when you're a business owner who now has to adapt almost on an hourly basis to new guidelines and regulations. When I get upset, I throw myself into work and work as much as I can. This is not a healthy coping strategy, and I don't recommend it. But for me, it allowed me to focus on something else and keep myself so busy that I wouldn't have time to do much else. I was dealing with internal guilt and depression, but I didn't let myself show it because I had to keep the pharmacy running and be there for all my staff and my patients during the troubling times of early 2020. I would work 12-hour days (or longer), come home, go to bed, get up, and repeat again the next day. To me, this was a way I could cope. I also decided to remain positive, and since I got pregnant so quickly the first time, I assumed I would again, and I'd be pregnant again in a matter of months. I was so naive; nothing really of worth is ever easy.

The weeks turned into months, and I still wasn't pregnant. And that just wasn't fair. How could others get pregnant so easily, while I had to struggle? How could I be happy for my friends and employees who got pregnant when secretly I was so jealous of them that they would get to become a mother, and I was just over here waiting. When you're trying to get pregnant, you start living your life in two-week cycles; Part One: waiting for ovulation and Part Two: living super carefully and cautiously while waiting to take a pregnancy test. This is how I lived in 2020. I'd start testing for ovulation around day 9 or 10, so I didn't miss the window. And I kept checking daily until I ovulated, and then the second two-week wait would start. The early pregnancy detection tests—I just skipped them! They were always negative, so I had always hoped that it was just too early to detect. I don't even want to think about how much I spent on pregnancy and ovulation tests that year. Then I started getting frustrated as I reached the one-year-of-trying mark. I was now 30, and in pregnancy terms, that's old, and your chances of getting pregnant are going to start decreasing as the odds start to stack against you (well that's how it feels). Not only do you feel guilty that you can't get pregnant, but you feel so upset that, as a woman, your body just can't do its one basic function: to create life. That feeling is heartbreaking and depressing.

At the one-year mark since we'd started trying to get pregnant again, my doctor referred me to the fertility clinic. Since we were still in the pandemic, there was a bit of a wait to be seen, but luckily, fertility treatments were not classified as "elective treatments," and I was still able to be seen (they just couldn't see as many patients as previously). By January 2021, my fertility blood work was completed, and I was booked in for a sonohysterogram. This is a test where they literally fill your uterus with a saline solution while doing an ultrasound. It will look for any abnormalities in your uterus and ensure that both your fallopian tubes are open and not blocked. I was told that this test would be uncomfortable, but I could take an Advil beforehand, and I would be fine. Uncomfortable is an understatement! I've always suffered from horrible period cramps, but this was like the worst case of cramps times 10, and I almost passed out from the pain. Due to the pain, they couldn't properly finish the test, and the results were inconclusive. That meant I would have to do the test a second time the following month. The second time, I took more Advil prior to the test and a lorazepam so they could complete it.

This time, the test was a success in that they were able to get results. The results weren't the best news, as they showed that my left fallopian tube was blocked. How or why it was blocked, they didn't have an answer for. It just was. Apparently, when you ovulate one month, you'll ovulate on the left, and the next month, it will be on the right. I'd been through pharmacy school and had never known this. This meant that if my body did what it should with ovulation, I would only have a chance to get pregnant every other month. Since trying naturally wasn't working, the fertility clinic's suggestion was to try IUI (intrauterine insemination), but we wouldn't be able to go any further with that until my husband completed his tests that they needed.

Trying to get a man to see a doctor is like pulling teeth—it doesn't go over very well. It took months of convincing him that everything could be perfectly fine with him, but we wouldn't know until the results are in; and that by thinking the worst, it was just setting us up for a further cycle of the unknown. The number of times I also had to explain to him that I couldn't even get monthly ultrasounds to see what side I was ovulating on until he had completed his blood work was numerous. Men hate doctors. Let's just throw that out there and make that a well-known fact! While I was waiting for him to complete his "stuff," I decided to pay extra to get an AMH test done. An AMH test is a blood test that will tell you approximately how many eggs you have left in reserve. The results of this test showed that I had the egg reserve of a 37-year-old, and I was only 31! This was devastating news to me. I had never felt so aged in my life. I also had never hated the way my body had functioned so much until I got those results. I felt betrayed by my body. Had I caused this to happen when I was a teenager with my eating disorder and not thinking of the future? Had I caused this by keeping my phone in my pocket or using my laptop in my lap (I still don't know if there is any evidence behind this)? Was this due to stress? A low AMH level means that you want to have fertility treatment/get pregnant as soon as possible if having a child is your goal. Luckily for me, this was a huge factor in getting my husband to finally complete the tests that the fertility clinic needed because they told me I should get my name on the IVF waitlist as soon as possible due to the low egg reserve.

This brings us to September 2021. I had somehow made it through a full year of managing a pharmacy through a pandemic, I had immunized hundreds of patients against COVID-19, I had gone above and beyond to ensure our local camp staff were vaccinated to allow for summer camps, but I still wasn't pregnant. I was also beyond tired. Work was catching up with me, we could not keep staff on, I could never make everyone happy, someone was always complaining, and customers were always mad! I was trying to please hundreds of people a day and was now working over 12 hours a day. I would only show up at home to sleep for a few hours and then return to the pharmacy to try to catch up. I wasn't living a life that was making me happy, and I hadn't been for a while. I was still dealing with guilt and disappointment from the miscarriage, but I didn't know what to do with it.

September 2021 was also the date that my unborn child would have turned 1 year old had I not miscarried. The feelings were real, and they hurt a lot at this time. I remember thinking for a period of time that had I not miscarried, I would be celebrating my baby's first birthday, but instead, September 2021 was the first month that we were finally able to start our first cycle through the fertility clinic. I was finally beginning fertility treatments!! I was so positive. I thought, "I'm seeing a fertility doctor now. Things are going to work out right away!" Famous last words. Let me tell you how seeing a fertility clinic works: Day one of your period, you call the clinic and let them know your period started and that you want to complete an IUI cycle with them. Based on your period history, they will call you back and tell you what day your first intrauterine ultrasound will be (usually somewhere around day 10-12). This ultrasound will give them an idea of what side you're ovulating on, and how many follicles are developing. You also have to complete blood work to ensure all the hormones are within a certain range. Luckily for me, my first cycle that I called them to start an IUI, I was ovulating on my right side (if it was the blocked side, there would have been nothing they could do for us that month), and all my blood work was within range. This meant that I would be going for an ultrasound every other day to monitor the growth of the follicles until they reached a certain size (in mm). Once this size was reached, they gave me a syringe to give an injection to myself and explicit instructions on when we were to have sex, and then they told us what day we were to show up at the clinic with a sample.

We followed their instructions and showed up on our appointed date and time for the IUI procedure. The setup for the procedure (where they pick the best sperm from the sample) literally took longer than the procedure itself. Once the sample was ready, the doctor came in, and in less than two minutes, the sample was inserted. You then lie down and rest for 10 minutes to increase the likelihood of a successful procedure and then you're on your way. In 13 days, they schedule you in for blood work that will give you an answer within 3 hours. I came out of our first IUI session feeling so positive.

I felt that there was no way that this wouldn't work. After all, it was based on science, and as a pharmacist, I trusted the science. This began another two-week cycle of waiting. I was so careful with everything that I did, I sat down as much as I could at work, I didn't have a single drink, I avoided processed meats, and since I was doing all the right things, I was so sure I was going to get that positive test result on day 13. I just felt that the first IUI was going to work for me. Boy, was I mistaken when I got that call a few hours after the blood work and again felt devastated and started questioning myself as to what I did wrong. This was based on science, how could it not work? What was wrong with me? I told myself I would be depressed and sad until my period started again. We would try again next month. It would work for sure next time! I let myself have a few drinks, a few cries, and then pulled myself together because sometimes that's all you can do.

A few days later, my period started, and I called the office again, super excited that we could try once more! We booked the next appointment for about day 10 of my cycle, and I couldn't wait as I just knew it would work this time! I showed up to the ultrasound, and the tech told me that I was ovulating on my left side. I asked her what this meant, and unfortunately, it meant that no IUI procedure would take place for October. I asked if there was anything she could do or if I could do something to make the clinic change their mind; unfortunately, the answer was "no." I went over to the clinic with my test results, almost in tears, and begged the nurse if there was anything at all she could do. Again, the answer was "no," and all I could do was try again next month.

By October 2021, I was reaching my limit at work. I often had mini panic attacks during my shift because I was just so stressed out. I couldn't find full-time pharmacists that wanted to move to Parry Sound, I was having trouble finding pharmacy assistants to work full-time hours, and my staff were exhausted, but patients still needed their medications. I started working at 6am and stayed after we closed until 11:30pm some nights just to try to finish the daily tasks, so we weren't starting the next day behind schedule. I was playing the role of an owner, a hiring manager, a pharmacy manager, a pharmacist, a regulated technician, a pharmacy assistant, and covering shifts when staff couldn't make it in. I was dead tired, I couldn't think straight most of the time, and I would forget the most basic tasks; I was basically running on fumes day in and day out. I finally reached the point where I knew I needed to do something for my physical and mental health because I couldn't keep functioning (or lack of functioning) like this, and I also knew that this probably wasn't helping my chances to get pregnant. I did one of the hardest things for me, as a workaholic, to do. I called my district manager and told him I needed to take a stress leave because I was burnt out. I was able to take four months off to rest and destress and make a plan to return to work in a way that I could function. So at the beginning of November, I officially started stress leave. I slept for 18 hours a day for the first month!

November was also the third time I called the fertility clinic when my period started again. I figured that since I was off work, the IUI would finally happen! I showed up to their office for the early blood work (I think it was day 3 blood work), which would tell us early on if I could continue to a monitored cycle. I remember it being our anniversary night when she called back and said my blood work was "off" and I would have to skip November for fertility treatments. How could my blood work be off? I just went on stress leave and was feeling much better! She had no answer. In case you haven't figured it out yet, there are a lot of questions with no solid answers in regards to infertility. Although I was very disappointed, again, she was able to put my name on several waitlists to be seen in Toronto for an IVF assessment. I was ready to pay however much I needed to and as quickly as possible to get pregnant.

By some small stroke of luck, one of the IVF clinics called me and was able to do a virtual assessment late one night on a Saturday just a few weeks away. I agreed as quickly as possible and took the appointment. It was a two-hour, in-depth conversation with the head fertility doctor at the clinic to review all my blood work, all my test results, my husband's test results, and come to an assessment on what we should do to move forward. The summary of the call was that due to my low AMH levels, I should start IVF as soon as possible, but I would have to come down to the clinic for further tests that they needed from their office. I booked their earliest appointment, December 22, 2021.

We went down the night before and stayed in a hotel, so we wouldn't feel rushed the next day. I finally felt like we were getting somewhere! During the appointment, they took a lot more blood work to run further tests and did a lot of poking and prodding. I was told that right after New Year's, I would have a follow-up phone call to discuss the best route to start. I was sent home with a handful of vitamins and minerals and finally some hope!

During all this, my period had started, and my blood work was on target. I also had an ultrasound that showed I was finally ovulating on the right side again, and I was told we could certainly try a second IUI procedure this month. I was going to take all the chances I could, and we had the second IUI on December 27th. During the two-week wait for blood work, we had our follow-up call with the Toronto IVF clinic, and the best suggestion was to start IVF at the beginning of my next period. Since I had regular periods, I told them when I expected it to start, and they tentatively booked me in to be seen as soon as my period started, so we could begin the medications. I didn't think the IUI would actually work this time, so I was taking all the chances I was given. Finally, day 13 came, and I could go for blood work to test for pregnancy. I really didn't have my hopes up, and I knew that within the next week, I would be seeing the IVF clinic anyways, so things were moving in the right direction.

A few hours later, I got a call from the fertility clinic, and my blood work had actually come back positive! I was finally pregnant! I couldn't believe it! I think I asked her five times if she was 100% sure of the test results, and she reassured me that it was correct. She asked me to come in in two days to ensure my HCG levels were increasing as they should, and then we could get an early ultrasound done at six weeks. I was so excited! The next set of blood work showed my levels were more than doubling every 48 hours (which was great news). I asked at the clinic if I could begin progesterone shots to reduce the likelihood of a miscarriage again, and we agreed that

that was a good plan. I was to give myself injections daily until I reached 12 weeks. This would help reduce the risk of a miscarriage.

When I got this news, I decided I needed to make career changes. There was no way it would be healthy for me to continue to work in such a stressful environment while pregnant, and I didn't want to miss any of my child's early years. I handed in my resignation as an owner two weeks later and felt such a huge relief.

At the six-week mark, I was able to have an early ultrasound. At six weeks, the fetus is just a little mark on the screen, but I was able to hear a heartbeat! It was the best news ever, and I was so full of love! I continued to take it easy, and I switched jobs to work in a doctor's office part time, and for once, I felt less stressed. I was able to leave my work at work at the end of the day and focus on growing a human.

Certainly there is some mental work that needs to be done when you have a history of an eating disorder and you're pregnant. Your body goes through so many changes on a daily basis, and it can be overwhelming. You have to keep reminding yourself of all the amazing things your body can do and that it's literally growing a human being from nothing! Women are amazing! I asked the doctor's office to not show me my weight when I went to appointments and to only focus on it if there was a concern; this was respected. I had to remind myself daily that food was fuel for myself and for the baby. This was a reminder that really helped me get through some of the most difficult days when my mind wanted to play mind games with me. This is not to say the pregnancy was easy. I still had to deal with unbearable nausea for 16 weeks and extreme fatigue due to low iron. I required iron infusions and would still get tired easily. I rested whenever I could and took it easy, and I didn't feel bad about it.

Fast forward to the end of nine months of pregnancy, and my beautiful son was born. Finally, all the struggles were worth it! The delivery didn't go as planned, but as they say: don't go into delivery with a plan because it will be thrown out the window when the baby does whatever they want to do! They also say that a child born with a "stork bite" at the back of their head means that the baby has been kissed by an angel. This may be a superstition, but it's one that I choose to believe. I believe that our unborn child left their mark on the back of James' head as their angel kiss.

Chapter 9
KATIE WICIK

www.linkedin.com/in/katherine-wicik-m-ed-a9a53997/
@parentcoach2.0

Katie Wicik is a mother to three remarkable young people: two teenagers and one tween. She and her supportive husband continue to navigate parenting through life's transitions together. Katie has a passion for ecotherapy and values the therapeutic benefits of being outdoors and with nature.

Katie has over 25 years of mental health and addictions experience working in hospital, educational, community, and private practice settings. For the past 10 years, Katie has worked exclusively with parents, couples, and families. Katie offers specialized support and coaching for parent, couple, and family relationships where one member has a diagnosed pre-existing mental health condition. Katie has teaching and research experience in university, college, and hospital settings in addition to providing supervision to students. Katie has been a mental health specialist presenter and has been highlighted in various media outlets. Throughout her career, she has served on several boards of directors in addition to executive and philanthropic committees that have a focus on women and children, healthcare, and community. Katie completed the Couple and Family Therapy Studies Advanced Certificate with distinction at the University of Guelph and Canadian Association for Marriage and Family Therapy (CAMFT). She completed an M.Ed with distinction in special education and counselling from Brock University and a B.A. (Hons) from the University of Toronto in psychoanalytic thought.

PARENTING 2.0

Unpacking Parenting

"Unpack your baggage, so your kids don't have to carry it." — Lu Hanessian

Our relationships with our children sets the stage for every subsequent relationship our children will have in their lives. Through unpacking our own parenting styles, we are able to hold space for our own baggage (emotional/intergenerational/systemic) and consciously choose what gifts (values that we hold precious) that we want to pass on to our children and future generations. Parenting 2.0, in my viewpoint, is more about us as parents (our responses to our own triggers and problematic parenting styles) than it is about our children.

The following is my journey through motherhood and how I came upon parenting 2.0 after almost two decades of being a parent. It's been a journey that I imagine that I will continue to need to be flexible and adapt with each new life transition and struggle that my family will face. I have come to the understanding that I cannot take away my children's struggles, nor is that a helpful undertaking for both my children and myself, as much as I wish that I could at times. However, by holding space for my own baggage (emotional) and living my life using the gifts that I want to offer my children, I have come to learn that this is the most impactful thing that I can do as a parent.

Pregnancy Phase

I was embarking on the biggest, most exciting, and scary journey of my life—motherhood! I voraciously read all the parenting books (these days, that also includes scrolling through social media, blogs, podcasts, etc.) that I could find. The numerous 101 Pregnancy and 101 Parenthood books that I found offered me some basic knowledge and strategies that were helpful at the time, but the focus always seemed to be on "how to parent" as if there was one "right way" to do it. Subsequently, I spent the last 20 years or so learning and studying parenthood. If there was a right way to parent, I was determined to figure it out.

Parenting 101 has gotten me this far. Parenting 2.0 takes it one big step further. It explores the relational aspects of who I am as a person and what informs my parenting style, both in problematic and loving ways. It involves unpacking the baggage (emotional/inter-generational/systemic) that is part of my parenting style and prioritizes the gifts that I want to offer my children as well.

Newborn/Infant Phase

My entrance into motherhood was a traumatic one. I suspect most, if not all, are as we are thrust into this life transition. My first child was born into the world through emergency measures, which was followed by a week in the NICU (Neonatal Intensive Care Unit). It was a period of significant uncertainty, one of many more that were to follow, where my world stood still. Alongside the heroic healthcare providers, my husband and I did everything we could to ensure our newborn's survival.

Unbeknownst to me at the time, even in those mindful moments where every breath mattered, I was living out my values. I vividly remember a nurse asking me why I seemed so happy to be racing over to the NICU wing from the maternity ward where I was staying to feed my newborn baby. My response was, "How could I not be happy? My son is alive. He needs me, and I'm grateful that I am able to spend time with him and feed him."

"If we want to be a safe harbour for our kids, we can't be the storm ourselves." — Dr. Tina Payne Bryson

Eight days later, I was able to take my healthy warrior baby home, in huge part due to the extraordinary measures of the healthcare team who not only provided exceptional care for my son but also offered compassion, knowledge, and hope to us as parents.

Another three weeks later, I was in a state of complete exhaustion. I was determined to make breastfeeding viable, apparently even to my own detriment, as up until then, I had not realized that my own needs were also paramount in being a mother. I knew that breastfeeding was the best option for my baby, yet the NICU stay had added additional layers that made it all that much more difficult. I was stuck in an endless cycle of breastfeeding, pumping, and breastfeeding some more, which left literally no time in between to sleep or rest. When I conveyed this to my exceptional family doctor, Dr. W, who has been my family's hero on many occasions throughout our lives, her response was that parenting is holistic, and taking care of myself was indeed in the best interest of my son. Miraculously, the pressure to carry on in a manner that simply was not working had been lifted. Now, looking back, my family doctor's response sounds intuitive and logical, but at the time, I was determined to parent in the "right way," and I had not realized until then that the "right way" also included what was right for me as well. This moment proved transformative in how I parented from then on and planted the seeds to Parenting 2.0.

The practical application of all my 101 learnings about being a mother were shifting. My internalized expectations around what a mother should be like and my subsequent shame and guilt for already not fitting into this mold now offered a new freedom that allowed me to anchor in my own values, not what I felt society and parenting culture indicated I should or should not be like as a mother.

Fast forward almost two decades, and my first born is now a thriving, healthy, and brilliant young man who is an independent driver and whom I could not be more proud of. Those early decisions regarding breast or formula seem completely insignificant now. Reflecting back on my earlier motherhood years offers a beautiful reminder that when I am facing some of the most heartbreaking and soul-crushing moments of my life in 5, 10, and 20 years from now, it is certain to look completely different.

Tween Phase

Each childhood phase has brought its own unique celebrations and heart-aches. There have been many times since those early NICU days that my parenting world has stood still as I have navigated broken bones, broken systems, and broken hearts , most often my own. It was during the COVID-19 pandemic that my two older children went from being tweens during vari-ous states of lockdowns and quarantines to emerging out into the world as teens. Alongside other parents, I was quickly thrust to pivot and support my children in their new world of online learning in between my own virtual meetings for work. After weeks of lockdown, my children's bedrooms had become multipurpose spaces where they attended virtual classes, social-ized online, and sometimes even had to eat meals (during times when fam-ily members had to quarantine from one another).

Etched in my mind is the day that I went to check in on my daughter, whose white bedroom started to feel like a hospital room akin to what a patient might spend endless hours in. My childrens' world had necessarily become incredibly small during the pandemic, and I knew that how I navigated this new pandemic territory, which included taking care of my own needs, was a significant influencing factor on how my children would fare through it as well. Nature was our solace, as it offered a sense of normalcy and a change of scenery. Friday night home movie nights became a new tradition to offer something to look forward to. After a long period of hibernation and isola-tion, my two older children emerged as barely recognizable teenagers and my youngest as a tween.

Adolescent Phase

The days when I could not get a moment to myself to take a shower alone, the stroller walks, and the endless crafts and dress-up play are now distant memories. Those early childhood years when I was so engulfed in mother-hood that I wondered when I would ever have a moment for myself again are no longer. Things have shifted as my children now have full-time school and homework, part-time jobs, sports and activities, and beautiful relation-ships with their peers.

"As a parent, you quickly realize that life is one long series of letting go: watching your kid crawl, then walk, then run, and then drive away." — Deborah Mitchell

As my children are launching towards their own independence, I am finding a way to hold space. As a mother, part of this transition is also grieving those earlier developmental stages, when as parents, we were our children's whole world, and it felt easier to try to keep them safe. These days, I am learning to hold space for the quieter silences, knowing they will share on their own time as they, too, are figuring out this new life stage. I try to hold space for my parental baggage when it creeps up. I'm mindful that I cannot always protect them from what life will throw their way, but I can offer a soft place to land and to fiercely have their back when invited to. Every single day, I am in complete awe of my children and the faith they offer me in the next generations.

My children are leading the way, and I am in a continual state of trying to catch up and adjust to each new phase. After almost two decades of being my children's secure home base, I see my children getting ready to launch. This is what I have always hoped for them, yet I am simultaneously holding space for how painful it is, as their mother, to slowly let them go. My children still need me, but in much different ways than when they were young. I am sure they will keep coming back to check that their secure base is still there to help launch them further.

BAGGAGE (emotional/intergenerational/systemic)

"Parenting is hard because your child is reflecting back to you what you haven't yet resolved within yourself." — Nurture Parenting

For me, parenting 2.0 involves unpacking the baggage that is part of my parenting style and reflecting on the gifts that I want to offer my children. It offers me a space to reflect on why, as a parent, some things bother me and others do not. It is my baggage that can get in the way of how I want to parent, but it also invites me into a space to heal and move towards the parent I want to be instead of just reacting to what comes up for me. My parenting pattern, when triggered, is to go to a place of fear, back to those early days of parental expectations where I questioned if I was doing this right. My parenting block ignites as a fierce protector and advocate: How can I protect my children from the world's and life's struggles? Bearing witness to our children's suffering is one of the most painful things we can endure as a parent, and how we manage our own emotions that come up around this are key.

GIFTS (Precious Values)

"Our values connect us with what is in our control: the ability to act like the sort of person we want to be." — Russ Harris

The gifts, the precious values that I hold dear and that I hope to offer my children, are what will give them the freedom to navigate their lives in the way that suits them best. The gifts that I want to offer them include prioritizing their own needs (including health), family and friends, passionate work, and a sense of fun and adventure. I continue to lean towards relationships that fuel me and allow me to enjoy the beautiful village that we are so blessed to have surround me and my family.

"The quality of our relationships determines the quality of our lives." — Esther Perel

Chapter 10
MICHELLE HARRISON-FAULKNER
@faulknermommy

I grew up in a generation where lots of little girls just think about being a mom when they grow up; the rest doesn't matter. When I was little, I used to play "house" with my dolls. I had an older blonde female doll and two baby twin dolls (male and female). If I tell you that now I have an older light-haired bonus daughter and two biological children (son and daughter) that are only 15 months apart, you would think I manifested this. I like to say that I first became a "mom" in an unconventional sense, but there is no "wrong" way of becoming a mom, whether it's biological mom, adoptive mom, foster mom, stepmom, surrogate mom, etc. When I met my now husband, knowing he had a daughter, I had never even dated someone with a child before. I knew to keep boundaries, but I fell for him. When I knew for sure that I wanted him to be my forever, I understood that he came as a package deal—and not just with his daughter but his daughter's mother as well. Occasionally, I say that I wish someone would have told me then what exactly that package deal entailed, but I'm glad no one truly scared me off.

I met my bonus daughter when she was just 16 months old. Now at seven years old, she lives primarily with us and has since she was three. I was a motherly figure to her immediately. I understood (and still do understand) that I am not her biological mother, but I refused to use that as an excuse to not be a mother to her. I changed her diapers and made her bottles when she was a baby, I care for her when she's sick, and I cook her meals. I help her with homework, prepare her school gear, and help her navigate how to be a good friend but not be walked all over. I could not fathom treating her like anything but my own, but I understand that some stepparents need to keep that kind of distance for a wide variety of different reasons. Being a stepparent is definitely not for the faint of heart! I'm lucky that I can do what I do, despite the challenges. Being a bonus mom first definitely changed my experience of becoming a biological mom.

I believe that the experience of being a stepparent is directly influenced by the relationship the biological parents have and also how the other biological parent thinks of you. Regardless of that, you get to choose how you are going to handle yourself. My initial experience while dating my now husband was not positive. There were calls to the police, there was harassment, and everything in between. I tried to stay positive and tried not to let it phase me. I knew that this was the man I wanted to be with, so we kept on. The beginning of our relationship feels like a blur. It wasn't the "typical" getting to know each other phase. We lived together almost right away. He was already a parent, and that was our focus. We also were involved in the family court system almost right away. This involved legal paperwork, court appearances, police calls, etc. Our relationship was serious from the beginning, and I was blunt: I was not getting involved and falling in love with a man and his daughter for this to just be a fling. I knew he and I were well matched and that we were either serious or kept our distance; thankfully, we chose the first option.

I also knew that I wanted to have children of my own, and he wanted more children, so we started to try and get pregnant. As we began our journey, we were grateful to quickly get onto the Ontario IVF waiting list (as my bonus daughter was an IVF baby). After a few months, though, we found out we were pregnant! It was the one-year anniversary of the day we started talking. I know, we moved quickly! What's funny is that my stepdaughter had just started calling me "Mom" after an extended visit (10 days) with us while her mom was traveling, and it coincided with when we became pregnant. I often say she knew before we did!

I had just deactivated my Facebook account because the harassment from the other biological parent had become so bad. So I wasn't able to share with family and friends (that I didn't speak with regularly) that we were expecting. And I remember how not-so-kindly the other biological parent exclaimed that it was good that I kept my pregnancy a secret, and she wished I kept it more of a secret. When we announced to my mom that we were pregnant, the first words out of her mouth were "Ohhhh, [she]'s going to be a big sister!" My extended family and I have always loved my bonus daughter as if she were born into our family. Our whole world was about our children as it has been from the beginning.

During my pregnancy, my husband was deep into family court. He was self-representing (meaning we did not have a lawyer), and we did all the paperwork throughout the whole process. It was during my final trimester that we prepared thousands of pages of documentation in preparation for an 11-day trial. That was the most exhausting experience of my life. I was so ill after testifying that I broke out in rashes; we had to pause the trial. I had been diagnosed with gestational diabetes a week before the trial, but was unable to schedule time at the clinic to learn what I was supposed to do. I simply monitored my sugars. I prayed that would be enough and that I wasn't harming my baby, but my attention was more on the task at hand than the beautiful miracle growing inside of me. To be totally candid, I didn't put much thought into my pregnancy, the birth, or having a newborn at all. I obviously prepared to have a baby; we had planned this pregnancy. So we picked a name and we got the crib out of storage that we had packed away from my bonus daughter, but I didn't think about a birth plan or whether I would breastfeed or not. I didn't take the time to read the books or just sit in the glory of being pregnant. I wasn't able to plan a babymoon vacation or relax and enjoy my final "pre-baby" days leading up to my son's birth.

Sometimes when I look back at all the things I missed out on during my pregnancy with my son, my first child, I'm sad. I look back and grieve for the experience I always imagined I would have. I'm sure other women have felt this way for a variety of reasons, but this just felt so beyond my control. I could not control the players in my story or even have control over which players would have so much influence. Looking back as a wiser woman now, I wish that I would have worked on controlling what I could. I could have taken more time to sit and read the baby books if I wanted. I could have just taken the time to go to a spa or stay somewhere overnight with my partner before the baby. These are all things that I was just too overwhelmed at the time to think were within my reach. Had I taken a step back, I would have seen just how capable I was to do them. I enjoyed being pregnant and feeling a baby growing inside of me. I even enjoyed that slow waddle that drove my husband crazy at the end of my pregnancy. When I look back, I try to concentrate on the positive experiences.

After the May family court trial, there was more paperwork to do, and the deadline was only two weeks before my due date. All paperwork was submitted just on time, and on July 6th, I became a biological mother. Even my birthing experience was tainted by the fact that my husband and his ex couldn't get along. When my husband had to drive over an hour away to pick up his daughter, I wondered, "What if I went into labour during this time? I would be alone, or rather, without my husband. What if he missed the birth of his firstborn son?"

We were advised to try to induce labour approximately 10 days before my due date. It was horrible, and it did NOT work. Side bar: I am absolutely blessed that my husband advocated for me with the doctors, and when they made suggestions, which seemed like demands, for things I didn't want, he stood up for me. Your body, your choice! At the end of that experience, we elected for a c-section, and to be fully transparent, this was the best-case scenario. It wasn't left to nature, and I knew that I went into the hospital at 5:30am for a 7:30am c-section and by 8am, I would have a baby! Thankfully, despite very relaxed prenatal care, my son was born absolutely perfect. I was happy that my birth experience worked out for me because I know not many do in this type of situation. All I can suggest is to make back-up plans and back-up plans to those back-up plans. For us, that was keeping my mom and family in the loop and on the ready in case my husband couldn't be there. And when he had to complete the first exchange, my mom was with me.

I think one benefit of being a bonus mom first was that it allowed me to have a more relaxed birth and newborn experience with my son. I always assumed I would be a nervous helicopter parent, yet I had this underlying confidence when I had my son. Sure I hadn't taken care of my eldest in her first year, but I knew some of the tricks that most "first-time moms" don't. I was also much more confident, thinking to myself that my husband would know all the answers because it wasn't his first time. This is one of the blessings of being a stepmom first.

Becoming a biological mother is definitely a different experience than becoming a stepmother. I carried this baby, I fed this baby from my body, and I co-slept with this baby, to name just a few ways it was different. But don't let whether you experienced pregnancy or even the first year(s) of a child's life or not dictate your role. My bonus daughter is so important to me, and oftentimes we talk about how even though her brother (and now sister) grew in my belly, she grew in my heart, and she's quite content with that explanation.

After giving birth, I was aware of postpartum depression and other things I may feel or experience, but I do wish someone would have warned me about the experiences my husband might have. I didn't really think about it; he was already a dad, so what difference would another child make? But it did. He was now a full-time dad to his son, where he wasn't able to be with his daughter full-time. He could feed and bathe his son every day; he couldn't do that with his daughter. He spoke with, played with, and put his son to bed every night, and he didn't with his daughter. In addition, this child was a boy. My husband does not have a good relationship with his father, and so the thought of being a father to a son really wore on him in ways I cannot even fathom. My husband and I would have benefitted from some more preparation for this. I wish we were aware of resources for him as we were told of many for me as the mom. I wish someone would have warned us of the whirlwind of emotions that would be felt. Blended families are different for everyone, and the men are impacted just as much as the women. There likely are starting to be some resources out there, especially since COVID-19, but it's been so taboo for men to talk about their feelings, and even the divorced family resources are not geared towards men. We really need to advocate for the mental health of our men. There are some great men that need the support just as we moms need support.

It took months for my husband to be comfortable with having another child, and during that time, I was adjusting to being a full-time "first-time" mom. One thing I haven't spoken much about to anyone was this overwhelming fear that my son wasn't mine to keep, that someone was going to take him away. After going through family court and having no control or say over the life of my bonus daughter, I found it very hard to believe that wasn't going to be the case with my son. He was my baby, and I was always going to protect him. Just as we were getting into our groove, we received what felt like the most devastating results from trial. Although many things were achieved, the overall result was not what my husband and I had hoped for. I think it was harder for me than for my husband. We had put so much work in, but we didn't have the luxury of having a lawyer; that was an expense we couldn't debt ourselves with, not with a baby on the way and having just purchased a house for our family. Thankfully, the lawyer we had for advice didn't take advantage of us and insist on representing us. As awful as this experience had been up until that point, I reflect on all the wonderful people we came into contact with, whether it was professionals or other people experiencing similar issues. I have to say that the group of step-mom friends I've made have gotten me through it all. Having a safe space to vent and bounce ideas off of like-minded individuals helped me stay sane during the darkest of times. After getting those results, I thought, "Will this instant matter in five years (and if not, don't give it more than five minutes of your time)?" At the time, it felt like it would, but being five years down the line now, it really didn't. Eventually, we used the saying, "It is what it is" or my current favourite: "This, too, shall pass." I tried to convince myself that maybe in five years, these results won't matter. But in reality, even a year later they didn't!

Very quickly after receiving results from the trial, our situation changed entirely again. My bonus daughter's biological mom reached out and wanted to work together. Now let me explain as bluntly, honestly, and kindly as possible that this was not a wonderful epiphany. I don't think she woke up one morning and thought, "Maybe my ex-husband's new wife isn't the issue." She needed our help; she was not well. And like that, my husband and I didn't think twice. We jumped to help, both feet in, head first, into the fire, and we helped wherever we could and likely more than we should have. Looking back, the word "boundaries" comes to my mind.

For the next 9 months, my bonus daughter's biological mother and I were like best friends. We texted all day every day, she slept over at my house for the May 2-4 weekend, and I arranged things to ensure she could sleep over in September to see our daughter's meet and greet with her teacher and her first day of school the following day. She was one of the first people I told when I found out we were pregnant again. My son was only six months at the time, and we told her as we were all out together celebrating Family Day. She even came to my OB appointment months later to listen to my daughter's heartbeat. It was nice to have this time when we were all coming together, but as they say, if it feels too good to be true, it might just be. My husband and I saw warning signs. We knew that, unfortunately, before we started getting along, she had been placing the blame all on us when she spoke with her support system. As such, they gave her a hard time when we were coming together. In fact, they were not supportive of our newfound friendship and co-parenting arrangement at all. Here's one such example of this: a few months into our friendship, I had been trying to arrange a lunch to celebrate and support her and the battle she was having with an autoimmune disorder. There was a walk, but she didn't want to attend because she was having a hard time, so I suggested I could arrange a lunch before or after the walk with her family and friends to support her. Her mother and a large portion of her other family and friends told her they refused to attend if my husband and I were going to be there; they missed that this coming together was not just for the child, but for her mother, too, who needed us to come together. And, to be honest, I can't understand that. We had been to her mother's for dinner, had her father over to our home for dinner, we had celebrated events with her boyfriend, heck, we even had our daughter's fourth birthday party as a big group at her dad's house. We were open, honest, and raw, and apparently that wasn't enough. When something went wrong, someone had to take the blame, and that someone was me and my husband. When finally the pressure from the lack of support from her support system erupted, we were the ones to take the hit.

As much as it was nice to experience this kind of co-parenting, it added a layer to the grief. It's difficult. My bonus daughter got to see all her parents getting along and coming together for her, but when it imploded, she was just a victim of the aftermath, not understanding why her biological mother used to sleep over at our home and then refused to come to events for her. She couldn't understand why exchanges used to be laughing and taking selfies, and then they became tense and sometimes involved arguing or happened at a police station. A hard lesson was learnt here. Regardless of what the future holds, this coming together that we had will never be our future. We will always maintain boundaries because the one that suffered was that little girl, and that wasn't fair. And even years after this implosion, I still grieve for it. I still sometimes pick up my phone and think I should text her a picture of our daughter's hilarious outfit she picked out, how well her printing is getting, or just something funny that happened. It pains me that she misses these moments. And briefly after the implosion, about a year into the drama, we tried again. And we did text and act friendly, but it was short lived. Someone must be the bad guy in the story, and the "evil stepmom" just fits the bill.

Ultimately, I grieve, wondering if this was all a game for her. Despite those raw conversations we had, I can't help but wonder if she meant any of the apologies given. I wonder if she understands how much I cared for her. I really thought she was a true friend and that we were parenting together. We were parenting a beautiful, spunky, intelligent, and kind little girl. If I could go back, I don't know that I would have changed it. I was open and honest, and I wanted her to know how much I love that little girl, so much so that I was willing to be there for her biological mother. There was no expectation for us to help, but we did. I was (and often still am) helpful to a fault.

I often try so hard to see the good in people that it's hard to understand that some people just don't. It is important when in a situation like this to set clear boundaries of what you're willing to do and what you're not. And what saved me and my family was documenting everything. I mean put EVERY-THING in writing and track, log, and save it! Because when the shoe dropped and the situation reversed again, we weren't left just scrambling to pick up the pieces. As I mentioned, my two biological children are very close in age, so a lot of this back and forth occurred during what should have been precious times in my early motherhood. I was able, for the most part, to enjoy my pregnancy with my daughter before this implosion. There was no family court or stress in this regard; however, we used to joke that I was taking on another child—my bonus daughter's biological mom. She wasn't working and needed help to get forms filled out, to keep track of medical appointments, to remember schedules, and to have overall emotional support. And it was during my second pregnancy that it was determined that my bonus daughter would move in full time with us to attend school, so there was paperwork with registering her for a school in our area, legal paperwork, and just getting everything organized. And it all needed to happen very quickly!

We went from having my son full time and my bonus daughter part time to having three children full time in mere weeks. And not even a month after that, we were back in court. The implosion of our friendship with my bonus daughter's biological mom brought even more drama and difficult experiences.

Exactly a year after we'd received those devastating results from the trial, our situation was vastly different: our bonus daughter was living with us, which is what we strived for, and we have another baby (born on the 1-year anniversary of the final court order, no less)! You could not have convinced me when we received those results from the trial that a year later, it would all be so different.

But for those who have had the pleasure of not experiencing family court, please try and understand how absolutely devastating it can all feel being in and out of family court for six years. I was 7 months pregnant while preparing for and testifying at the first family court trial, my son was only 3 months when he entered a courtroom for the first time, and my daughter was only 3 weeks when she entered a courthouse for the first time a year after that. My wedding was tainted by the fact that the very next day, my husband's ex started another unfounded war against us, with calls to the police and Children's Aid Society, and an unsuccessful visit to the courthouse; this resulted in months of people coming to and into our home. My children are growing up thinking it's normal for police to stop by the house or call Mommy and Daddy's phone (and this hasn't stopped).

When I try to explain it to intact families, they are shocked at how long family court takes—hours to get paperwork together, days of missed work for court appearances, and YEARS before any decision is made, and not even by you, but by a judge. A STRANGER decides how you are going to live your lives! For those who have experienced family court, especially if it's at all like my experience, please maintain hope and good faith, although depending on your personal experience and situation, having hope can be so difficult. A lot of people give up, but there is hope, and there are good people out there that can help you with the experience.

And finally, for those who are thinking that they might need family court, please do everything in your power to stay out of it: mediation, parenting coaches, co-parenting coaches, arbitration—anything! There are so many resources and courses to try and co-parent and stay out of family court. It really isn't built for the best interest of the child. I will always advocate that you need to make sure that your spite and hatred for your ex (and/or their new partner) never outweighs your love for your child.

As I write this now, my youngest daughter has just turned three, and we are currently preparing for another family court trial. Yes, that means it has taken three years to get to trial, although some of that is because of COVID-19 delays. By the time this book is published, maybe we'll be living the results! I am also dealing with more unwarranted and unnecessary police involvement—just another tactic to try and break us down. This time around, though, we are older, wiser, much busier with all these kids, and we've learnt a lot of lessons. Most importantly, though, I'm happy that no one convinced me not to take on this life. It isn't easy, that's for damn sure, but what part of motherhood is? And before I had kids or even before I had to deal with co-parenting with a person I didn't pick as a partner, life in general wasn't easy. There is always going to be something that's hard. And this thing—it's just one thing.

I look at intact families that don't need to deal with all the extra stress, and I realize that they, too, struggle with basic survival sometimes. No matter what you deal with, it isn't about the "what." It's about the "how." HOW do you deal with these struggles? Whether it's co-parenting, problems in your relationship, boundaries with your in-laws, work troubles, friend troubles, etc. Ultimately, your state of mind is controlled by you. Despite the family court, the drama, missing out on the pregnancy experience with my son, missing out on the newborn experience with my daughter, parenting a child who isn't biologically mine, the fact that I have to consider that there's a whole other family that comes along with my bonus daughter—despite all these things, most of which are outside of my control—it is about how I look at things.

I, just like you, can find joy in every moment, even the tough ones. You can find the lessons, and better yet, you can pass those teachings onto your children, who will then be better equipped for the world and all its troubles. Every single person's experience of life is different and unique. Yours is what you make it, so whether you need to spend time in a courtroom or not, whether you have a great relationship with your parents or you've cut them off, whether you have easy children or those who need more connection, whether you are parenting or co-parenting with a narcissist or you have a great parenting relationship, none of it changes the fact that you can choose to have dance parties with your kids, have ice cream for dinner, or a movie marathon while snuggling and eating snacks. You can choose to be the best parent you can possibly be. You can shamelessly be yourself.

You can choose to take time for yourself or anything else you choose to do. All that drama and trouble—it's just one part of my life. Sure it affects a lot, but so do I. And some days, I'm just surviving like the rest of you. Some days, the problems seem like too much, and I need a mommy time out. But most days, I choose to take control.

I choose to control my life, to show love effortlessly, and to maintain healthy boundaries. But most importantly, I choose to do my best to raise kind, brave, funny, and creative children. I choose to enjoy little moments, to soak in all the experiences with my husband, children, and extended family, and I choose to be the mom I want to be, no matter what anyone else tries to say.

Chapter 11
REBECCA RECHTORIK

rebeccarechtorikrecovery.com | @rebecca.jaay

I never wanted to be a mother. I was, in fact, vehemently against it. But the truth is, I didn't think I could be a mother; I didn't think I SHOULD be a mother.

I am Rebecca, and this is my story.

I consciously decided many years ago that I was not fit to be a mother. My mental health never felt stable enough to plan for any type of future that required consistency; it felt irresponsible to daydream about someone relying on me, when, in all honesty, I couldn't rely on myself.

I was sick and raging a war against myself, and the battlefield was my body.

Body image. Those two words, when standing alone, don't mean much. Together, they can influence your life in the most profound ways. I have vivid memories, branded into my consciousness, of times that body image limited my ability to interact and engage with the world around me.

Too Young to Remember: My nana gave me a Christmas present: a cute set of cotton undies and a bralette top. I cried. I do not even know why it made me feel so shameful and embarrassed.

Grade 2: I was far too uncomfortable to wear a crop top. My mom bought me a cute little set of shorts and a crop top with bright neon colours all over them. I wouldn't wear the shirt because my tummy showed. We fought. The compromise we reached was the shorts (which were tight) and a large, oversized cotton t-shirt with an Aladdin scene on it (Jasmine and Rajah).

Grade 3: Sports Day. Shit. Swimming, with the entire school as bystanders. I stood on the bleachers in my bathing suit, dying inside. I desperately tried to quickly change back into my school uniform afterwards, still damp and sticky from the chlorine, but trying to undress/redress under a towel, so as not to let anyone see my body. My shirt got stuck on my head, and I started getting more sweaty as panic set in. I wondered how I would be able to do this without help or dropping my towel, so I could use both hands to get dressed.

Grade 5: I insisted on wearing a one-piece bathing suit under capris and a t-shirt at a pool party. I watched the other girls and pretended I did not like swimming. That was easier than admitting I was ashamed of my body.

Grade 6: I wore my brother's and dad's hand-me-downs. They were big, baggy, and long. Right as baby doll tees started emerging, I was drowning in fabric. I wore a black toque, tucked all my hair into it, and did my very best to look like a boy.

Grade 7: My dad bought me a present: denim shorts and a spaghetti strap tank top. I was so excited to unwrap the gift and absolutely devastated when I saw what was inside. I would NEVER wear either of those items. I was consumed with the idea that my cellulite (I had none; I was 11) was on display, so I covered up with Champion tear-aways. I thought that if I could hide it, maybe no one else would see all my shame. The feeling of sweat drops speeding down my back underneath the thick maroon cardigan I favoured (a hand-me-down from my brother) was uncomfortable but manageable compared to the distress of showing my body.

Grade 8: Britney spears. Christina Aguilera. Low rise everything. I borrowed my brother's super awesome orange and navy board shorts. I envisioned them hanging on my hips, looking effortlessly cool. I could not even get my older brother's shorts to go up over my hips. I was drowning in shame.

Grade 9: I wore sweatpants on the beach because I was too embarrassed of my legs to show them. I was too embarrassed that I had my period to participate in anything. Instead, I sat on the sidelines, sweating and pretending I was fine.

Grade 10: Miss Sixty jeans. I fucking hated those jeans. They were tight, form fitting, expensive, and they showed everything. It seemed as if everyone was wearing a size 26. I didn't fit into a size 26. And my parents couldn't afford this brand. I swathed my body in black Champion hoodies and XXL sweatpants.

Grade 11: Who the fuck knows? This year was a blur. This is a lost year when my eating disorder absolutely and completely took over my entire life.

Grade 12: I sobbed in my closet with the door closed and the lights off, jeans stuck on the swell of my thighs. I took sleeping pills during the day simply to escape myself. I spent hours in front of the bathroom mirror squeezing, sucking, stretching, grabbing, and checking. I hated every single thing I saw.

College: I was unable to walk through the classroom door on the very first day of school. I was convinced that everyone was staring at me, judging me. I could feel their eyes on me, analyzing my body; their gaze was palpable. I was wearing light blue Dish jeans, bright green Converse high tops, a hoodie, and a jacket. I was underweight. I felt as though I sucked all the air, all the space, out of the room. I dropped out shortly after.

My Twenties: Hey, my dad is dying from cancer. I went to visit him in Vancouver and refused to have my picture taken because my face was too round and my cheeks looked fat. He's gone, and we have so few pictures together.

I could keep going. I have countless memories like this, of distress and discomfort. I was always shrinking, but never small enough to feel safe from judgement. I don't have a lot of memories of what else was happening during those times.

I have binged, purged, and restricted myself in an effort to control my body. I've taken uppers to suppress my appetite and give me energy when awake. I've taken downers to make me sleep because at least I didn't have to think about food when I was asleep.

I've abused alcohol to navigate social situations. It made me able to detach from reality and the fear of what people thought of me. I've done Cross-Fit, bodybuilding, powerlifting, P90X, Beachbody, BBG, yoga, running, MMA, boxing, kickboxing, and pilates, chasing the "perfect" body with zero regard for injuries or rest.

I've been vegan, vegetarian, high fat, low fat, no fat, no carbs, Paleo, Whole30, IIFYM, clean, raw, gluten free, sugar free, dairy free, keto, and every single other diet plan known to mankind, all in an attempt to have the perfect body, so I could be "good enough."

All of that is the reason I never wanted to be a mother. My days were filled with working out, weighing food, and hating myself. There was no air, no space, for any joy, any connection, and certainly no capacity for motherhood. I knew I couldn't model anything I wanted her to learn; I was not a role model. And this was not a life I wanted to pass on.

The messy healing came next. Unlearning and recreating the belief system that made me sick and rewriting all the stories I held about health, body, food, and worth seemed counterintuitive to everything I knew. I had been promised that I would feel good about myself if my body looked a certain way. But, putting so much value on how I looked only caused anxiety and degraded my self-esteem.

The ONLY thing that has made me comfortable in my own skin is this: healing my relationship with food and letting go of trying to control and manipulate my body. Letting go of that has been what allows me to feel at home in my skin.

I'll admit it; even after treatment and years into recovery, even when I had come to a fragile truce with my body and had begun to know it and accept it for what it was, not what I wished it was, pregnancy just seemed like too big a leap into the unknown.

It felt like too much to sit with and accept a changing body—the body I fought with and the body I worked so hard to control, shrink, and "maintain." How could I possibly be alright with a growing body? An abdomen that swells, hips that get wider, breasts that get bigger, and an overall softness to my being... Every single one of these things are what I had fought adamantly against since puberty.

And then I got pregnant. And I was doing it. I was accepting my body, a body that was growing, changing, swelling, and softening. And it wasn't the end of the world. I sat with it. I accepted it. This body, this unrecognizable body, is still MY body.

It is still a good body and an acceptable body.

Motherhood

I see so much of myself in my daughter: how she thinks, how she reacts, and the enormity of her emotions. In many ways, I parent her the way my younger self needed parenting. When it comes to disorder, there isn't one factor, no single cause to point out. Genetics loads the gun, and the environment pulls the trigger. I cannot influence her genetics, but I do have influence over her environment. Cycles get passed on so innocently, so automatically—but the cycle of self-hate and body shame stops here.

So now, everything has become intentional: every decision, every action, and every rule. Everything that I am aware of that can "pull the trigger" and is within my control, I am intentional about. What my daughter sees me eat, how she hears me talk about food, or how she sees me treat my body is all very intentional. I am a big believer in intent and impact. These are the two components to explore in our decisions—what is my INTENT/MOTIVATION to do this, and what is the IMPACT on my/her life if I do this?

My daughter will not grow up believing her body is a problem to be fixed. She will not witness a mother at war with herself. She will not inherit the belief that her body is shameful, wrong, or needs to be hidden.

My daughter will see me in a bathing suit. She will watch me wear shorts and participate in every activity, no matter what my body looks like. She will watch me try new things that I am not good at, while I laugh at my mistakes.

My daughter will never see me step on a scale or pine over a certain body type. She will never see diet products in our fridge or hear me speak unkindly about my body.

My daughter will know that my body is my safe place, that I trust my body, respect my body, and celebrate its function. My daughter will see all of these things so that she may learn to trust her body, too.

"As they get older, our daughters become more and more like us, too." — Amy Newmark

Will you be satisfied if she feels the same way about her body that you do?

At some point, in every family, it becomes necessary for cycles to be broken so that our next generation can be unburdened from carrying limiting beliefs.

Chapter 12
ROSANNA SPADAFORA

rossanamias@gmail.com

My mind is seldom quiet. I tend to overthink things, and years ago, I was very hard on myself. At my worst, I'd nitpick at something that happened or a thought that came to mind, and I'd scratch at it until I was raw. I spoke with someone about it, and they provided me with the tools I needed to bring some peace to my mind, and it worked. But once my baby was born, those tools were misplaced as I shifted my priorities from myself to my child.

I can honestly say I was not prepared for motherhood, despite my efforts. Like most first-time moms to be, I tried to consume as much information as I could while I was pregnant in hopes that when the magical day came, I would feel confident in my abilities as a new mom. I was constantly reading books and articles, I participated in online courses, and I took birthing classes. From what I gathered, motherhood fit into this sort of box. The box contained the classic joy and excitement, overwhelming feelings of love and worry, sleep deprivation upon sleep deprivation, self-sacrifice, saying farewell to multitasking, figuring out when you last showered, and somehow still being able to feed yourself in addition to your new little family member. "It will be hard, but it will be worth it. My hospital bag is packed, the nursery is stocked, meals are in the freezer—Let's do this! I'm ready!"

Then I gave birth to my beautiful boy, and what started to unfold was unlike anything I read, unlike anything I saw, and unlike anything I have ever felt.

During my pregnancy, I never gave much thought to what my mental health would be like after the fact. I had read little snippets about postpartum depression here and there, but it never occurred to me that it would be part of *my* new-to-motherhood experience. Right as we were about to leave the hospital, the nurse in the mother and baby unit spoke with us: "Have you had issues with depression before?" to which I replied, "No." "Do you know the signs of postpartum depression?" Thinking of the simplified version of PPD that television and movies taught me, I said "Yes." She then proceeded to tell my husband to be on the lookout for said signs. I should have taken her concern more seriously, but I chalked up my emotional breakdowns to the fact that my baby was born with a heart condition, and we were cooped up in a small hospital room during strict COVID-19 rules for four days while we waited for his testing to be completed. Plus, you know... I just had a baby; it's an emotional time.

Our first week home was overwhelming, obviously. I'm not even going to mention sleep deprivation anymore; let's just assume it's ever-present and unrelenting. We were adjusting to our new life. I was healing and desperate to bond with my child, but having visitors every day felt like it prevented us from having that time together. Although I welcomed literally anyone from the outside world, I felt like they were getting the opportunity to bond with my child while I watched on the sidelines. It did not help that everything I read beforehand hammered that crucial bonding experience into my head. If I don't bond with him now, what's going to happen? Will he not love me? Will he want someone else? I am messing this up already! The self-induced pressure to bond with my child was building, but there was minimal relief. I wanted my baby, but I had no voice to cry for help, so I just cried alone in silence.

Over the next couple weeks, I started putting myself down again, fixated on everything I was doing wrong or couldn't do, and I questioned my capability as a mother. For every "why is he crying?" remark from family members, my mind twisted it to "why can't you comfort your baby?" With every concerned look, I saw "do you even know what you're doing?" written across their faces. And with every "tsk" rung in my ear, I heard "that poor baby!" My mind created what felt like a thick fog of judgement. With every "concern" they had, my mind warped that concern into a question of my fitness as a mother. I then started comparing myself to my sisters. Motherhood seemed so effortless for them, so why is it so hard for me? They're bonding with their babies so naturally, so why am I struggling? Their bodies are producing breast milk, so what's wrong with mine? She's on her third child, she's on her second, and I can't even handle one? The fog got to the point where I could no longer see. Harsh thoughts were bombing my mind 24/7 until I deemed myself hopeless, and it consumed me.

The cruel thoughts had not stopped. They only got worse. I began fantasizing about how peaceful death would be, how my mind would finally shut up and leave me alone. I'd sigh at the relief. In all the messiness that was in my mind, it didn't click that this line of thinking was a problem. Of course, I never said these things out loud to another person. I kept it to myself and let it fester. The longer I kept it to myself, the more it became a secret. Ah, such bliss: me, baby, and PPD makes three! But you know the saying "three is a crowd?" So PPD invited her lesser-known friend, postpartum anxiety, and made it a party—the kind of party where drinks were solely made of tears, and ominous music was playing on a loop.

Within the first few weeks home, I had my first panic attack. This is when my mind really took things up a notch. I was going to pump in the baby's room while my husband had him downstairs. I was really looking forward to this time alone and had built it up in my head. For 20 minutes, I could finally put on Netflix, watch something uplifting and mind-numbing (the keyword here is mind-numbing) and quiet my mind. Mistakenly, I did not tell my husband how much I needed this. He came into the room shortly after, sat beside me while holding our son, and proceeded to chat (God bless him). I could feel the dread overcoming my entire body. I finished pumping, stored my milk, and sat down to eat. While my husband put the baby to sleep, I started shivering uncontrollably, teeth chattering and all. I didn't know what was happening, but I just kept thinking, "You're never going to escape. You'll always feel like this." It played on repeat, like it was taunting me. My husband came in, scared out of his mind, and wrapped 3 blankets around me as I shivered, "I'm so cold." He was going to call 911, but I asked him to do breathing exercises with me. The deeper the breaths and more focused breathing I did, the less I shivered until it completely stopped. We were both frightened in disbelief and utter confusion as to what just happened. Instead of telling my husband what I was feeling before and during what I now know was a panic attack, I kept it to myself. At this point, my husband began seeking answers, but I did not... That was, until the following week.

It was one of those days. I couldn't stop crying. Everything I was doing was wrong (in my mind). My husband was late for an appointment for work, and I was pumping. We got into an argument over my fleeting sanity and inability to admit that something was wrong, but he had to leave, so he did. I was alone with my son and just finished pumping a whole 1.5 ounces of disappointment, only to bump the table the bottles were resting on. Whoever coined the saying, "Don't cry over spilled milk"—James Howell, a man— clearly never experienced the complex feelings of breastfeeding. You want to be able to feed your child from your own body as done by women since the beginning of time, but you know that your body and, by extension, you are letting your own child down. Even though you've eaten the right foods and consumed "magical" elixirs, nothing is working. Still, you're holding onto hope that you'll be able to turn it around (see, complex). So yeah, I cried over spilled milk. I picked up my child, sat on our rocker, and gave him formula. As I sobbed over my baby, telling him how much of a failure I am, my stress levels peaked. I could not move. My arms would not budge; my hands were glued to my child. It was as if I was frozen in a state of shock, which of course caused me to panic more. There I was, alone with my child who was now screaming at the top of his lungs because he wanted comfort, and I was immobilized, watching him suffer. I had to use Siri to call my husband (no answer; in a meeting), my mom (no answer; babysitting), and finally my brother, who answered.

I am very grateful to my big brother. I was incoherently crying, saying I needed help, and he simply replied, "I'm on my way." I'm also grateful to my husband, and this is the only time I'll say it, for installing all things technology in our house, including our door lock and door camera. As soon as my husband saw my brother racing up the driveway and through our door, he knew something was wrong and rushed home. My brother took my son and placed him in his crib. He sat down and asked me what was going on. It was odd to have a conversation about breastfeeding with my brother, but I told him what had happened. I told him about the struggle I'm having with it and how it has ended with me in a frozen state. Both my husband and mother had arrived during this conversation, and what they all said was true: the only person pressuring me to breastfeed was myself. I omitted everything else regarding my mental health because it was my "shameful secret." I eventually made it off the chair, but my arms could not move, and I could barely make a fist with my hand. The next day was the same. For three days, I could not pick up my newborn baby, and once again, I had to watch everyone else hold and nurture him. All I wanted to do was hold my baby, but I had failed. I was failing as a mother. I'm not bonding with my child, my body is not producing milk, I can't nurture my baby, and my mental health is plummeting.

Then I had a moment of clarity. I thought back to the conversation I had with my brother, mother, and husband; it had me questioning what was really going on with me, if breastfeeding was worth the exchange for my well-being, and why I was deteriorating as a person. Thankfully, my husband and mother pushed me to go see the doctor even though I was reluctant to talk about it.

I went to the doctor to discuss my anxiety and my breastfeeding struggle, but I could not muster up the courage to say that I am having intrusive thoughts, I can barely function, I am an empty shell of a human being, I do not recognize the person I have become, and I need help. My mind was yelling, "Help me!" But it could not escape through my mouth. It was obvious to the nurse, the doctor, and my husband who accompanied me that I did, in fact, need help. The nurse talked me through letting go of breastfeeding and the societal pressures of "breast is best" and encouraged me to embrace "fed is best" instead. I understood it had to be on my own terms and that a sort of grieving process would need to take place for me to feel comfortable in my decision to stop. She also gave me a script to read from whenever I felt the anxiety boiling up to the point of catastrophe—and it worked. The anxiety became more manageable over time. The doctor gave me information for clinics specializing in PPD and asked if I would like medication to balance me out, but I was hesitant. For me to accept medication would mean there is a problem. But I was in denial. It could be a million things, but it's not postpartum depression.

I could not admit it to myself. I can't tell you how many times I've googled symptoms of PPD. I made so many excuses for my actions and reactions to justify that what I was feeling was "normal." The fact that I kept going back to search it should have been my eureka moment, but I downplayed my degenerating mental health. It wasn't until about 4 months after my visit to the doctor that I accepted it, and I remember the exact moment. I was driving alone. Typically, this is a happy place for me. It always has been. I blast my music and get lost in it. But on this day, there was no music, and I was just sitting in my thoughts (more like drowning in them), and the fantasy of how peaceful death would be crept back in. Then it was as if reality had personified, slapped me across the face, grabbed me, and yelled "wake the f**k up!" That evening, I finally admitted to my husband that I needed help. It took me six months to say those words out loud, and it took me another six months after that to seek it from my doctor. Even though my husband had been telling me to call the doctor for months, he couldn't force me to do it. I had to first accept there was a problem, and if that problem could not be cleared on its own, then it was time to get outside help.

For me, medication was not an option at this point. After admitting I needed help to my husband, I decided to tell my mom about everything I had been feeling over the last six months. Of course, she knew something was wrong during this time, but because I never said it out loud, she tried supporting me in different ways and would keep me in check when I put myself down. When I opened up to her, I realized that I was brewing negativity from all ends. I was letting fear overcome love, and the only person that was judging me unfairly was me. She encouraged me to build my confidence and drilled "stop comparing yourself to others" in my head until it hit.

Admittedly, things did get better for a while after these conversations with my mom/therapist. One source of my anxiety was family gatherings due to the self-created judgement I feared. I then decided I was going to protect my mental health while trying to heal it, and I stayed away from family gatherings during this time. I began to create boundaries for myself, and I was more vocal about the things causing me anxiety. Slowly, my confidence started to build. The more confidence I gained, the kinder I'd be to myself. My son and I were bonding more than ever. When I started to attend family gatherings again, the thoughts I once had became quieter. But, when something "bad" would happen—like my son getting sick or refusing to eat or we'd forgotten something of his at home—it would trigger that negativity and send me spiraling again for a week or two. The last "bad" thing that happened ended with my son and I locked in my parents' bathroom. I cried inconsolably, causing an almost panic attack and the intrusive thoughts to come back. As I talked myself down from the panic attack, I finally said, "Enough is enough. Get help." And I did.

I know I took the longest road possible to recovery. I could have prevented myself going through the wringer if I had admitted there was a problem. Maybe if I didn't feel so isolated in my feelings and struggles, I would have had the courage to seek help sooner. I realized I was mostly alone when I would converse with other mothers. They'd ask me how I was doing, and I'd always respond the same way: "It's hard, and I'm struggling." But their reply was never one of understanding or connection. I'd get brushed off and sometimes "laughed" at. Out of all the mothers in my life, I've only had one friend have an open and honest conversation with me about her PPD. I wasn't a mom yet, so I could only empathize with her, but I'm very grateful and proud of her for opening up and talking about it. It's not easy. When she asked me how I was feeling, I had no fear of judgement; I knew my feelings would not be rejected. But those dismissive remarks made by the people closest to me made me crawl into a deeper hole, alone. The thing is, if you don't get out of the hole, you're going to be buried in it. Your partner and loved ones can throw down a ladder to save you, but ultimately, it's your choice to grab it. And it starts with knowing you're not alone; there are millions of us.

Part of the problem is that PPD is not openly talked about amongst women. I was 19 years old when Brooke Shields shared her experiences with PPD, and I wasn't even sure what it was, but I remember everyone being up in arms about how she made her struggle public. People went as far as shaming her for it. I don't think that stigma has ever gone away because there has always been this biological narrative of motherhood = happiness. It's marketed as such. We see it in movies, television, ads, and even social media. A blissful mother is a good mother. In movies and television, a mother suffering from PPD is detaching from her child and "neglecting" her motherly duties; this is an "unfit" mother (not everyone experiences detachment. I don't know why they only choose this depiction of PPD). That stigma gets reinforced every time we consume something of that nature, not just for mothers, but for everyone. This is why I was in denial. This is why I was ashamed.

When I have been open and honest about motherhood, I get responses like, "You should be grateful you have a beautiful, healthy child!" I am grateful. Not once did I say otherwise. I have also been told, "Snap out of it! You have a baby." You're right. I'll just go splash cold water on my face, and all my problems will magically disappear. That stigma prevents women from sharing the darker side of motherhood. So, to answer the question, "How's motherhood treating you?" with a response other than, "It's great!" feels like a faux pas. You're too embarrassed or too ashamed to admit that it's hard, and sometimes it's so hard, it's unmanageable. Consequently, these women, myself included, walk through life with an invisible wound. And that's no way to live.

There is a need to normalize postpartum mental illnesses. If it were normalized, we would finally have a well-rounded representation of what motherhood is like in all its forms. If it were normalized, women wouldn't neglect their mental health for fear of being labelled or judged as an "unfit" mother. If it were normalized, seeking help would be more accessible, and that is very much needed because it is crippling to take that first step while you're this vulnerable. If it were normalized, you'd see the percentage of women who suffer postpartum mental illnesses increase because they would have the support, and thereby strength, to find their voice. Motherhood is not one-dimensional, and it is definitely not what you see on social media.

We've made many strides in mental health awareness and acceptance, but I feel like we've dropped the ball on postpartum depression, anxiety, rage and psychosis. Mothers who are experiencing any of these need to know they are not alone. I am fortunate that my friend talked to me about it because it caused a ripple effect. She talked to me, I'm talking to you, and maybe you'll get the courage to talk to someone else. That is why I will continue to be real with anyone who asks me about motherhood. You know yourself better than anyone. If you know in your heart of hearts that something is off, act on it. No one needs to suffer alone. There is absolutely no shame in asking for help when you need it; it may be the bravest thing you'll ever do.

I'd just like to thank my husband, my mom, and all my family for being the best support system I've ever had. Without you, I wouldn't have found the strength or courage to carry on. I love you.

Chapter 13
STEFANIE FERNANDES
www.stefaniefernandes.com | @iamstefaniefernandes

The Unsolicited Advice That You Actually Welcome: Healthy Boundaries as a Mother

Parenting is part of our humanity. Every single person on this Earth has experience in either parenting or being parented. That also means that everyone is an "expert" in raising children, or at least, they like to think so! I am certain that you have been on the receiving end of unsolicited advice since becoming a mother and probably even during pregnancy.

"You can't even imagine how your life will change!"

"Enjoy sleeping now; it will all be over soon."

"Enjoy the snuggles. In the blink of an eye, he can walk, and you won't have a restful minute anymore."

"Your life will be hijacked. You better get used to it now while you're pregnant!"

"I can see you still have your pregnancy weight. Don't eat that second piece of pie."

"How will your child learn consequences with your gentle parenting method? She manipulates you. You better show her who is in charge here!"

We have all received, and still continue to receive, unsolicited advice from close friends, family, acquaintances, the bus driver, or the cashier at your local superfood store that often crosses the line, and most of the time, it's actually not helpful.

I bet you can add a few more things to the list. I certainly can!

My name is Stefanie Fernandes. I'm a mom of 2 boys, and we live in the land of the happy people, Denmark, together with my Portuguese husband. Today, I want to give you the advice I wish I received when I was a new parent. This is the unsolicited advice you actually need and will actually help you improve your current situation and prepare you for future situations.

My advice is based on my own experience and my work with hundreds of mothers as a therapist and parenting coach. And whoever I talk to, it seems that it's a topic that concerns every mom, whether you are an adoptive mom, a single mom, a working mom, a co-parent, a bonus mom, a young mom, a rich mom, or a poor mom. It really doesn't matter. This is something we all share, and today, I will share my piece of advice with you.

It's something that we need to hear when we are pregnant and when we just had our baby. When our kids start preschool or when they start having sleepovers, this advice will help you and your child. It certainly helps me and my little wild vikings. Let's dive into it!

The Awakening

One of the biggest things I've learned in the past 6 years of being a mom (yes, I do include pregnancy as part of being a mother) is that it's so important to find your own way with yourself and your kids and to find your own way of parenting and living a happy life. Only you know what the right way for you and your family is. Most of the time, we don't know what the right way is for us, but we certainly feel when it's not.

We are looking for support and guidance. We are looking at how other mothers do it and how our mother did it. Google becomes our go-to advisor regarding sleep and feeding patterns and answers to questions like:

"Is it normal for my child not to roll over yet?"

"How much tummy time does a 4-week-old need?"

"What are the benefits of baby-led weaning, and when should we start?"

"What about sleeping through the night?"

"Is she growing enough?"

"How do we find intimacy again in between baths, diapers, sleepless nights, regressions, leaps, visits, loneliness, and burp cloths?"

And the biggest question I've had since I became a mom is:

"How do I emancipate myself from familiar family patterns and set clear boundaries that are in line with my own family values now?"

I didn't even know where to start. The advice I got before my son was born and in the first year of motherhood was mostly useless. (Sorry! Not sorry!) Google turned into my personal advisor. I didn't feel comfortable asking my friends or family the hard questions.

Why was that, you ask?

In hindsight, I think it was a lack of trust. And I didn't want to seem vulnerable. I didn't feel comfortable exposing myself and hearing even more of, "Well that's what motherhood is, so you better get used to it" and "Life is not fair, being a mother is not fair, and you can forget about your own life for the next 15 years."

I had days where I couldn't shower because my baby wouldn't sleep without being held, days where I didn't eat well, and many days where I didn't leave the house. I craved connection. I craved being held like my baby. I craved to be seen. But at the same time, I created that isolation I was feeling. Now I know that this is called avoidant attachment, and it's not my personality.

Living abroad means you gotta do it alone. And because it was my choice to move abroad and have a baby in a foreign country, I thought I couldn't complain about any of it. This belief was instilled in me for decades. "Your decision; your fault; you deal with it." Tough, I know.

That was when I realized that my belief system was not wired for duality. It was not wired for gray areas but rather for black and white: "You chose this; you better get used to it."

Acute postpartum is tender. And for me, it was the start of experiencing, and later on cherishing, the duality of motherhood and life. It is something so profound that I am still in the process of learning and accepting it even today.

I gave birth in a foreign country without speaking the language. I was far away from the place I grew up and without family close by for support. I gave birth, and advice like, "Motherhood is so natural. You will know what to do and how to do it" hollowed in my mind. Where exactly is that natural place? I must have missed my turn at the right intersection to arrive at that place. I certainly wasn't there right away.

Nothing in the whole world can prepare you for the moment when this new human moves into your house. If you have kids, you know that. If you are about to have your baby, you will soon experience that. I didn't ask for the advice that would actually be helpful before the birth of my first child. I was not conscious enough to ask the hard questions, the spiritual questions, the painful questions, or the deep questions. I was living an unconscious life. I was not prepared for the valve of emotions this new little human would open in me. Motherhood was and is still truly a portal of generational healing and growth for me.

The hardest part for me was to get through the days. There were days and days of loneliness. Cocooning wasn't tender for me; it was like a sticky mess that I couldn't wash off. Since I was not aware of where it comes from and how to deal with it, it didn't even occur to me that I could just surrender to it. I certainly didn't like it, but couldn't shake it.

I didn't understand the advice, "Enjoy the snuggles while it lasts; they grow up so fast."

What the heck does this even mean? I am here with a newborn who only sleeps on me. I can't eat properly, I can't shower, I am alone with him for most of the day, the week, and the month, and I feel so out of alignment, out of place, and out of my body, even though he is what I wished for.

When you are in the thick of it, in the fog, in the mental mud, you can't see where all that is coming from. What is going on here? Google doesn't validate and explain well enough because you are not really friends. You have no family close by to ask, your mom friends from your local mother's group are also in the thick of it, and frankly, they have no energy to spare on your soul-searching questions. Where does one even start?

Once the intrusive thoughts became stronger, and I got really scared and didn't recognize myself anymore, I decided to see a therapist. Not only did I want to be free from those terrible, terrifying thoughts, but mostly I knew that I didn't want to live like this. How could *this* even be sustainable for another week? I needed to start living a life that feels right to me. What feels right to each of us is different. Comparing myself to others made me feel inadequate. I thought that everyone loves motherhood, and I couldn't enjoy this right here. There is something wrong with me.

At one point, 5 months into motherhood, it became clear to me: This is not the life I wanted to live, and an invisible force pulled me to a vision I didn't even properly see yet, but I felt it. Little did I know that my emotional state had so much to do with my lack of boundaries. And this is where my unsolicited, actually helpful advice comes into play for you.

Chances are high that you bought this book because you want to have honest and real input from other moms. Maybe you want to get inspiration on how to deal with the impacts of parenthood. Or you want to prepare yourself. Maybe you have a sister, a daughter, or a friend whom you trust enough to share this chapter with. I trust it will land with the right person at the right time.

If there is one thing I have learned, it's that we moms should never ever hold back in telling our story. Somebody will benefit from this, and I sincerely hope that by telling you about my experience, I can give you hope that you can find your own way in the midst of the emotional roller coaster called parenting.

My Human Design

Humans are designed to be conditioned, and our conditioning starts from the day we are born. When we are mostly negatively conditioned, we lose ourselves. We live out of alignment, and we're not really the person who we are meant to be. And when our society and our parents don't see us for who we are but who we should be and how we should be, irrespective of our true nature, we lose touch with ourselves.

While on the search for who I truly am without the negative conditioning, I came across Human Design and discovered that I am 1/3 projector with a defined spleen and root. All my other 7 centers are undefined, which makes me prone to conditioning and being influenced by other peoples' opinions and emotions. I could see that I easily absorbed other peoples' energy and was prone to people-pleasing and avoiding conflict. These undefined centers provide insights into what I am here to learn in this life. Oh boy, there is so much to learn. This is my purpose.

This isn't your regular conversation about motherhood. It surely wasn't for me. Honestly, I am not even sure I could have understood it, absorbed it, and reflected on it in my early stages of motherhood. I wasn't ready. If you don't feel ready, if this doesn't land with you yet, give it time. Remember my words and come back to it. Read this chapter again and observe how my message lands with you then. There is a time when Human Design finds you. Maybe today is your time. Or maybe not yet. It is ok in any case.

I am having this conversation with you now because it turned my life around. It totally shifted my mindset. And it helped me to navigate my new role as a mother with more validation, with more trust, and with more depth. Then, something incredible happened. I became aware of my boundaries, and all of a sudden, I could change what I never saw before.

Most of us have a love-hate relationship with boundaries. We all need them—conscious and healthy boundaries—but we don't like to enforce them. They feel scary and unfamiliar. If they feel scary, don't shy away from them. This is not the type of fear that keeps you safe from the sabre-toothed tiger. Remember: boundaries are here to keep relationships, not to break them apart.

If you are a mother, you know that energy is precious. Raising kids is exhausting. There are days where I am drained at 8:30am, where I zoom out, where I am touched out, and where I am so tired that I can't answer one more "But why mommy?" question.

Giving love and attention constantly depletes me, especially as a projector, and I know you can probably relate to how high the energy is with two small kids who are hungry for love and pancakes.

Now what are healthy boundaries? What does this even mean?

Healthy, Scary Boundaries Are Not Dangerous

By telling you my story about how I found my personal boundaries that support my mental health and underpin my parenting, my aim is to provoke a discussion and create awareness. I am talking here about my own personal experience, about seeing my experiences and making sense of them through my lens of reality. This is my take on healthy and necessary boundaries, and it might differ from how you see it. Please take what resonates and leave what doesn't.

There are several different types of boundaries, such as emotional boundaries, physical boundaries, and financial boundaries. I was financially independent at a very young age. In hindsight, I can see now that this was my green card for independence. Working a job while doing my nursing degree and moving in with my then-boyfriend in my teenage years were both early efforts that set my boundaries. Feeling that invincible pull towards independence was present at a very early age for me. And I followed that pull successfully. Having that financial independence made it possible to take big life decisions in my own hands.

Financial boundaries are of paramount importance, especially for women, considering the disadvantages that come with traditional gender roles and how vulnerable women are without financial independence. I am aware that I am a cycle-breaker. I am aware that I am a cycle-starter.

Being financially independent and keeping up those financial boundaries were crystal clear to me. Financial boundaries allowed me to choose the education I wanted, to say "no" to an unhealthy work life and abusive managers, to sign up for therapy when I needed it, and to say "no" to a toxic relationship where I was as toxic as he was.

It's such an important foundation that I am fortunate to have established without even consciously realizing how absolutely game-changing it would turn out to be for my life and my children's lives. But when my son was born, financial boundaries were not enough anymore. I had to look at my emotional boundaries, my time boundaries, and my body boundaries. Chances are, you are a mother, too, and you can relate when I tell you how much personal boundaries change when you have a child.

Going to the bathroom all by yourself? Nope.

Showering every day in the first months postpartum? Nope.

Sleeping peacefully alone in your bed? Nope.

Having a romantic getaway with your husband? Nope.

If you feel postpartum is hard, it's because it is. If you feel raising little humans is hard, it's because it is. Having clear and healthy boundaries in place can help you navigate this phase of your life without suffering a tremendously heavy mental health burden.

What I came to realize is that I need boundaries to protect my energy and, subsequently, my mental health. My boundaries are my regular, daily self-care moments. And my boundaries support me in living by my values and living a life that feels in alignment and good for me.

Where Do We Even Start?

My boundaries are rooted in my values. I started with defining my boundaries after I saw how easily I can lose myself in other peoples' needs and expectations. I defined my postpartum as being a "good" mom, being a "good" daughter, and being a "good" wife. Others put their expectations on me, and I didn't know how to say "no" and how to create space for myself. Looking at my values (my personal values and my family values) really helped me to get clear and live in integrity.

I came to realize that I can never make everyone happy, and I let go of those expectations towards myself. For some people, it will never be enough—not enough time, not enough attention, not taking over enough tasks, and not saying the right things all the time. It's exhausting and impossible to constantly anticipate other peoples' opinions, reactions, and emotions.

The next step was to get out of the victim role. That required a mindset shift. I am putting these boundaries in place not because of other people but because of me—because of how I want to treat myself and how I want to feel, react, and respond. This has nothing to do with others but all to do with me. And that is the crucial piece of the puzzle that I feel is often disregarded.

I used to think that I needed boundaries because of other people. Truth is, I am setting boundaries for myself. As selfish as that may seem to you in the beginning, or maybe you are even triggered by me saying that, putting myself first and having healthy boundaries in place is the opposite of selfish. Only with healthy boundaries can you have healthy relationships that last, that are strong enough to overcome difficulties and disagreements.

Here is an example: When my son was just 2 months old, I didn't have boundaries regarding my emotions or my time. As a result, I went on a full-day sightseeing trip with visitors and a newborn. I didn't know how to say "no" to this. I was so glad they came to visit, but when they said we would be going around town, I didn't stand up for what I needed at that moment. I thought this is what I had to do to keep this relationship content and peaceful, to keep it intact. I had to please them, make them happy, and show my appreciation for their visit by disregarding my needs.

What I really needed was rest. I needed somebody who would help me with the laundry, cook me a nourishing meal, change my bedsheets, give me a hug, tell me kind words like "you are doing a great job," give me validation by saying something like "I can see that this postpartum phase is taking a toll on you; I see you," or simply ask the question "What can I do to help?"

Because I cannot expect others to meet my needs, I need to find a way to communicate my boundaries before the resentment grows, as hard as that may be, especially in times of overwhelm, stress, or growth.

When others didn't see that I struggled and didn't support me to feel better, my inner child responded. I was not the mom of a newborn. When my needs were dismissed and not seen, I regressed to being 5 years old. I felt the disappointment of a 5 year old, the unfairness, the pain, and the lack of cognitive ability to make sense of the situation. Being stuck in unresolved childhood experiences prevented me from setting and enforcing my boundaries. I need my cognitive ability to communicate clearly and calmly, and I need to align this with my core values, my feelings, and my needs. Only as both parts matured could these scary, healthy boundaries become my new support system.

It was paramount for me to mature, to process unresolved emotions, to heal my inner child, to love myself, and to empower myself. Only then was I ready to set my boundaries and communicate them. That took a lot of work, if I am being honest. It's scary, and it takes courage to step up. Becoming a mom helped me in that. When we become moms, we get that superpower, that unshakable conviction that we can do anything, especially hard things. That's what gave me strength to do the inner work and stop waiting for others to give me what I needed.

When working on your boundaries, it's helpful and important to know your attachment style.

If you have a disorganized attachment style, you know how difficult it is to deal with rejection. If you have an avoidant attachment style, you long for closeness but push people away, which can be quite confusing when setting boundaries. With every boundary comes the possibility of being rejected. Not everyone will agree with you. Not everyone agrees with me now. I learned that that is absolutely ok. It's safe for me. I am not going to die because somebody doesn't agree with me. I am not going to die. I am safe. I can never be rejected, because I will never reject myself. What an epiphany that was, and it solidified in a visceral feeling of emotional safety for me.

The Ripple Effect of Healthy Boundaries

I recently received a request from friends that they wanted to come to visit for 2 weeks. They would be staying in our house, getting up with us in the morning, eating with us, and spending the evenings with us. While I enjoy having visitors, I know that 2 weeks is too much for our family. The kids are tired after preschool and need time to wind down and re-connect with us as parents. As I am working from home, I need space to welcome my clients and be undisturbed for my calls.

Evenings are time to wind down for my husband and me. And they're also for chores we didn't manage during the day, like cleaning, tidying up, or laundry; and very often, they're for not doing anything at all. Evenings are also a time for me to hold my body boundary. I am simply touched out by the end of the day. I am too drained to talk, and I need to hold the boundary for my space. These are a few reasons why a 2-week visit at our place is simply too much.

"You are welcome to come stay with us, but maybe for a long weekend instead of 2 full weeks."

What an empowering and proud moment that was to say these words with kindness and conviction. By communicating our boundaries with empathy and kindness, we show others what is possible. We show other moms that it's safe to voice our needs. It's ok to disagree. It's ok to have different expectations. It's not about being right. It's about feeling well while doing this thing we call living life.

When we set and enforce our boundaries, we create a ripple effect that is not always visible for us in the moment or even in this life. It's especially hard to see the ripple effect it has on our children. Our kids soak up everything we do, hear everything we say, and constantly screen our nervous system. They do this to learn how to live and to learn what feels safe. When they are grown up, this will be their compass for relationships.

Communicating my needs ("Mommy needs a short break from talking now" or "Mommy goes for a walk to feel better.") helps me to prevent resentment towards my kids, but it also helps my kids to learn that it is ok to say what you need.

What I Have Learned Through It All

As I am navigating this parenting journey, doing things that I feel are right for me, I am aware of the need to make mistakes along the way.

There are things that I am learning to do without a blueprint, and you might find you need to do this, too. Having grown up not learning how to set healthy boundaries and communicate clearly and effectively with compassion and empathy, I recognize that there is always a part of me that regresses back to emotional immaturity. And that's ok. Instead of fighting it, criticizing myself, and being harsh towards myself, I am giving myself the grace of love.

I can have healthy boundaries for me that seem to be unhealthy for others.

I am safe communicating what I need even if it doesn't feel safe for others to receive.

I am strong and empowered even though sometimes I wish I could just crawl back into isolation.

Motherhood is all about this duality. Boundaries are all about duality. There are dynamics in play that you can't control. But there are dynamics within yourself that you can control.

One thing I learned, and I am still learning, is to communicate my boundaries in a calm and kind way. This is certainly not easy when my internal world is a volcano. The volcano erupts because of unhealed and unprocessed experiences. But even still... I am still growing and will probably never stop growing.

Have you ever wondered why there are people out there who bring up situations from decades ago? It's likely because they didn't process their experiences in those situations yet. And often, we need more than one occasion to heal the pain, more than one take.

Thankfully, because of my healing and growth, I can give my kids the space to process their experiences, especially when they feel my boundaries. They are safe to feel the disappointment over my "no," the grief over my decision not to have ice cream before dinner, and the sadness over a friend's decision to not come over for a play date. Everything is a process. Nothing is static.

Other people's emotions and needs are not mine to hold on to; these are my emotional boundaries. I can say "no" to a 2-week visit; these are my time boundaries.

It is still difficult, but I'll keep doing the work. I keep up with my boundaries because if I didn't, I would be drowning, and it would be impossible for me to be present for my kids and for myself. My presence, my wellbeing, and my parenting is so much more important to me than keeping the peace because others don't agree with my boundaries.

It doesn't get easier, but I get stronger.

Chapter 14

STEPHANIE GILES
@stephgiles11

Hello, I am Steph. I am a student, an educator, and a mother to two amazing children. My son is nine, and my daughter is three. My husband and I have our work cut out for ourselves when it comes to our children—one has ADHD, and the other is fiercely independent. They challenge me to be a better mother and educator every day. I have experience with mental health, both suffering from it and helping people suffering from it. I wrote a chapter in the first volume of *Honest as a Mother* (2022) regarding my journey getting my son diagnosed with ADHD, ODD, and anxiety. This time, I am telling you about my postpartum journey and the multiple surgeries that went along with it. This is a quick overview of what happened to me after the birth of my son.

I am sure you were told at least once while you were pregnant what a miracle giving birth is or how beautiful it is. I know I have. My first was far from a beautiful experience...

I had the most fantastic pregnancy with my son. I never felt sick—I felt terrific, actually—and I continued to work until my due date. About two weeks before my son came, I was already showing signs that my body was ready, and my doctor told me I would most likely be in labour by the weekend. Well, two weeks passed before my son was ready, and I went into labour around 3:00 am; by the time I could head to the hospital, it was about 6:30/7:00 am. Around 8:00 am, the doctor came in to examine me and said I should go back home. I told him what my doctor had said about my body showing signs of being ready, and he suggested I walk around the hospital, so I did. By the time I made my way back upstairs, my contractions were one after the other and were not letting up whatsoever. I refused to go home; I was in quite a bit of pain. The nurses helped me make my way to my room, and I begged for an epidural. When the anesthesiologist came, my anxiety went through the roof. I was scared. They asked my husband to leave the room, and I just cried. During the epidural insertion, the anesthesiologist told me I was her last patient, and she was sorry she took so long to get to me, but she had just found out that her best friend died. At this point, my internal alarm bells should have been going off, but I was in so much pain that I just needed something to take the pain away.

Fast forward to later in the evening, and my nurse was close to finishing her shift. I wanted her to be the nurse to help me give birth to my son because she was such a fantastic person and nurse. She came in and checked my progress. She indicated that I was almost ready, and by the time she left the room, my body decided it was time to push. I told my husband that he had to go and get the nurse because I was pushing, and I could not stop it. She came back and said, "yup, you are pushing." I continued pushing with the nurse until the doctors finally came in to take over. While pushing, I saw a group of TWELVE people come in. I remember pushing and thinking "Why are you guys here? Why are you all looking at my vagina?"

Suddenly, I was distracted by a burning feeling close to my clitoris. I pointed to it and asked why it was burning, and the doctor swatted my hand away and said, "don't touch it." At this point in my labour, with every push I gave, everything would go black, followed by everyone saying, "One more push! One more push!" I was getting so frustrated that I snapped at my husband and kept pushing. I never told anyone what was happening, and I should have. I finally pushed enough for my son's head to come out, and suddenly I felt him hit the back of my thigh. He literally had fallen out of me, and the doctors were not ready to have him come out, so they almost let him fall off the table! He was healthy; everything was good, except that six weeks later, we found out he had broken his collarbone, and no one had told us at his birth. But that's a whole other story.

When the time came to stitch me up, I could feel every stitch going in; I wasn't frozen anymore. I kept telling them, "It hurts, and I can feel every stitch." They tried their best to refreeze me, but they told me we were wasting time and they were almost done, so let's just get through it. It took FORTY-FIVE minutes to stitch me up. When they were finally done, I had a chance to rest a little. The nurse came back in and said, "We need to move you to another room, so we need to get you up and walking." The nurse asked me to stomp my legs many times and touched my thighs to ensure I could feel them before getting up. I felt her touch, and everything was fine. I got up, walked five steps, and my leg gave out. I was on the ground. We didn't understand why this had happened. I could feel everything, so why did I fall? Being who I am, I asked the nurse how bad the tearing was. She hesitated, but I was able to convince her to tell me. She responded, "It's the worst I've ever seen." The next day, my OBGYN came in and said, "When you have your next baby, you will have to have a c-section." I immediately thought, "I'm not having another one; I just birthed one! I'm exhausted!" But deep down, I knew I wanted a total of three children.

My son was three days old, and my husband was not feeling well. He had picked up C-diff and salmonella poisoning from the hospital. I was on my own.... with a newborn.... exhausted and confused. My husband could not touch our son; he could not help in any way. So there I was with a 3-day-old baby, a sick husband, and two giant dogs who needed to be walked. I did not even have the chance to take care of myself after having just given birth. I spent countless nights crying from being exhausted, from doing it all, and from having no one to lean on at midnight when I was at my lowest.

Around a year after giving birth, I started thinking something was wrong. I was wiping stool when I peed, and I couldn't hold in my bowels. My OBGYN told me I had a rectovaginal fistula the size of one millimetre. A rectovaginal fistula is a tunnel linking the vagina and the rectum. This tunnel can cause infections and incontinence. This one millimetre was the cause of my struggles with my bowels? And listen to this! My OBGYN was not allowed to fix it! I had to go to another doctor! The vagina doctor was not allowed to fix my vagina?! How does that work?? So off to another doctor I went. When I finally got in to see him, he said, "Yep, we will try to fix it; if we can't fix it, you might have to have an ileostomy." An ileostomy is a surgery where an opening is created in the lower right side of your abdomen, and the end of your small intestine is brought out to this opening. All waste passes through there and is collected by a bag.

Four months later, I got a phone call saying that my surgery to try and fix the rectovaginal fistula was scheduled for the next day. Perfect; that was fast! I went in and had surgery. Everything went fine, and I was recuperating. Ten days later, I went over to my mother-in-law's house, sat on her couch, and abruptly, I felt what it feels like to wake up first thing in the morning when you're on your period. I call it gushing. I went upstairs to the bathroom, and I'm unsure what happened or how I got there, but I ended up bleeding everywhere in the bathtub. I was rushed to the hospital and waited TWO hours—yes, that's right: TWO hours to see a doctor.

Imagine this: I was waiting in the waiting room, and I started screaming that I was gushing. My husband wheeled me to the bathroom and helped me get to the toilet. I had just soaked through my pants, and I felt ready to pass out. I told my husband to get a nurse; the nurse was very rude. She finally came to see me, and I looked up and saw her go, "Oh, no." I was finally rushed to the back to see a doctor. I was wheeled three footsteps away from the bed; I got out of the wheelchair and fell to the ground. The doctors had tried everything to see what was happening, but there was just so much blood—and it wasn't clotting—that I was rushed to the operating room. I was informed that they were only able to stop the bleeding. After I had gotten out of surgery, the doctor came to see me and said, "I'm sorry. You were just so badly infected. Your stitches had let go, and now you have a 2-millimetre rectovaginal fistula." The doctor that I had originally met with to fix this came in and told me that I'm going to need an ileostomy, and I had to have the surgery quickly.

I remember crying. Looking back, I am thankful that I had surgery so quickly because I was incontinent. One time was particularly traumatizing to me. I was on my way home from my mother-in-law's house, which was five minutes away, and by the time I got home and stood up, everything came out. I had no control at all. I walked upstairs to shower and just sobbed in my bathtub.

Surgery was a month later. I was so depressed in the hospital that the nurses were concerned about my mental health. The nurses called someone from the psych ward, and they came up and tried to help. It was challenging to understand that I was pooping in a bag. I was 23 and pooping in a bag. I couldn't believe it. When I got back home, I was seeing a nurse regularly to deal with my ileostomy, and she said to me, "I think you have a hernia." Having an ileostomy was horrible. I couldn't imagine having this bag for my whole life. Every day, everywhere I went, I had to ensure I had all my ileostomy supplies such as lots of bags (pouches to collect your poop) and flanges (this sticks to your skin, and the pouch attaches to it). There was one time at work that I needed to change it. So I took off my ostomy belt, and my full bag flew open. I was sent home because it was everywhere. Another time, I went shopping with my friend, and all I could smell was poop. My bag was full, and I had no supplies with me to change it. The shopping trip ended quickly, and I went back home. Having an ileostomy was one of the worst things that I ever experienced. I felt gross and smelly, like no one could ever love me again or continue to love me. My husband was supportive and by my side, loving me all the way. It was so embarrassing.

In my subsequent surgery, they fixed the rectovaginal fistula. I don't know how they fixed it, although they explained it to me at the time. I just don't remember. Due to my history of infections and mishaps with my surgeries, we had a nurse coming to the house weekly to see how things were going. On one visit, she told me, "Stephanie, you must return to the doctor because you're infected." If you've lost count, this is my 4th surgery (5 if you're counting the stitching from giving birth) in the span of seven months. And with each one, something went wrong.

I had to wait until everything healed to get my ileostomy removed and the hernia fixed. When I got the call, I was so excited that I would finally be able to move on with my life—or so I thought. I had the surgery, and the incision got infected. AGAIN. Over the course of the next year, I started to notice that one side of my stomach was growing yet again, and I was experiencing pain. I went back to the doctor only to find out that my hernia was back, and I had to go for ANOTHER surgery. Now, for those of you who probably have never had an ileostomy and hernia surgery, one thing they warn you about is possible bowel obstructions. A bowel obstruction is when your stool clumps together and cannot pass through your bowels. They warn you of obstructions after having surgery on your bowels because your bowels now have scar tissue and don't stretch like they used to. At my brother-in-law's wedding, I was in so much pain, but I couldn't figure out why, and I kept running to the washroom. It wasn't until a while after that I found out I had a blockage where my incision site was.

At the end of January, I went back to the hospital and had my final surgery. Everything was finally fixed, but that incision site got infected as well. My son was now four years old, and I missed out on so much of his life due to surgeries. In total, my surgeries took about two and a half years. That's two and a half years of not being able to pick him up, not being able to lay down on his bed, and not being able to read him a story.

Four months later, I was in so much pain and unable to walk. I ended up being so sick that my husband had to call an ambulance. Off to the emergency room I went. Again. I ended up being admitted and found out that my bowel was "possibly" nicked during my last surgery, and it was leaking. Over the course of the evening, I was struggling to breathe and had expressed it to my nurse. I remember waking up enough to see the X-ray machine and hear them say that I may need to be moved to the ICU. Thankfully, that didn't happen. I was informed that while being sick, I probably inhaled some vomit, and therefore, I now have pneumonia. After another round of antibiotics, I was feeling much better.

Six years after the birth of our son, we were finally able to welcome our daughter into the world. She came via c-section, and the incision did not get infected. YAY!!!!!! We took many precautions to avoid infections including having me on antibiotics for approximately fourteen days. My pregnancy with my daughter was nothing like with my son. It was not enjoyable. I had horrible back pain and hip pain. By the end of my pregnancy, my husband needed to take the last two weeks off work because I was unable to get myself to the washroom. He had to push me so my feet could slide across the floor just so I could get to the washroom in time. It was so bad that my husband and I decided that between the surgeries and my terrible pregnancy, we would no longer try for another child, although we did want one more.

I share this horrible experience because I want you to know that the afterbirth experience is not always fun and can be downright scary. There are so many things that can go wrong, but many women do not speak about these scary experiences. I spoke about what happened with my friends. Coincidentally, my one friend had a similar degree of tearing, and she reached out to me for advice. I am thankful that she did because I was able to remind her what happened to me and tell her what signs to look for. Thankfully, she did not have the same experience I did, but I was able to be there for her when she needed a friend who understood what she was going through. Afterbirth isn't always sunshine and rainbows, but if the only positive that came out of my experience was sharing it with others so they can prevent it, then so be it—Oh, and of course, my beautiful son that is funny, full of life, and puts a smile on my face.

Chapter 15
TOBIE KARST
@tobieelynn

Hi there,

Thanks for being here!

My name is Tobie Karst. I am a 29-year-old working mom. I have a lovely little girl named Peyton. In my chapter, we're going to talk about postpartum depression, a failed marriage, loss of a parent, the hardships of the journey, and how I have continued to overcome it all.

Let me start off by saying that I have had depression my entire life, so postpartum depression wasn't unexpected. However, postpartum rage, anger, and anxiety were a whole new level I'd never agreed to play. My postpartum depression/anxiety showed up as severe anger. I'm talking ridiculous emotional outbursts, physical outbursts, and straight up meltdowns. I punched holes in my walls and kicked holes in my doors. It was completely uncontrollable, and my mind went black with fits of rage. I was overwhelmed being a brand-new mother with no idea how to take care of a baby, as I'd never really been around one. I was alone due to it being peak COVID-19. My husband was a workaholic. I had such an odd and toxic relationship with my mother that even if she was around, it wouldn't have been helpful. She was also battling stage 4 skin cancer during that time. I was lost. I had so much love for my daughter. I never wanted to hurt her or cause her harm or pain. Being away from her was not often an option, and I didn't like the thought of that.

At about six months postpartum, my depression was so bad that I knew I needed help. Again, since it was during COVID-19, resources were stretched thin, and it was hard to access any type of help. The day I took myself to the hospital is still a blur. I told my husband he had to stay home with our child because I severely wanted to die. I told him I was going to drive myself to the hospital, and if I could walk up to the doors, I'd stay and check in. I remember walking through the doors. I looked at the receptionist with tears just streaming down my face. When asked why I was there, all I could say was "postpartum depression." I knew I needed the help. I knew I couldn't die. I knew I had to try.

Becoming a mother changed me in so many ways. I lost a huge chunk of who I was, I lost the man I vowed to be with for the rest of my life, and while learning to be a mother myself, I lost my own mother. Losing my mom left me feeling the most lost. My mother and I didn't see eye to eye (that story would be a whole book), but she was the one person who forever had my back, took me in when I needed it, and always picked up the phone when I called. I had lost the person I knew I could always turn to during the very times I needed someone to turn to the most.

Becoming a mother threw life in my face. It showed me just how much more I had to step up. It showed me that I had to try that much harder to live a life of fulfilment, to accomplish what I set out to do, and to heal from my own past. I needed to fix who I was in order to be the best parent I could be to my daughter—alone.

There was not one main thing that caused the breakdown of my marriage. Once I reached out for help, I just came back from that dark hole a different person. He and I weren't compatible anymore. The love was endless, and it still is, but being together as partners didn't make sense anymore. Separation didn't come easy, and the feeling associated with it broke me down in a whole different way. I sought the help right away this time. I knew the grief and the pain of not seeing my daughter everyday, being alone, and trying to navigate a new career all at the same time would feel impossible. Some days, it really did.

I woke up with panic attacks every morning. The stress was so severe that I developed an autoimmune concern. I struggled with weight loss and severe insomnia. Some days, I truly didn't know how I was making it. Most days, I questioned my worth as a mother, especially as a single mother to a 13 month old with no one to fall back on. I spent every day in fear. I needed something more. For myself to get better and be okay, I knew I needed to get real with myself, and I knew I needed more access to support and services.

This is where I began my healing journey, which is still a part of my everyday life.

I began more therapy, but specialized therapy this time. I started doing eye movement desensitization and reprocessing (EMDR) therapy and worked specifically with a grief professional who assisted me in overcoming and working through recent or stored grief. This was an 8-week process, but I still use EMDR in my everyday life when needed. Throughout those 8 weeks, I focused on learning, grieving, feeling, and eliminating, and I focused on myself again. I gave myself love daily. That was something I was really missing and truly craving while being alone. I was taught how to feel my feelings in a more appropriate and regulated way. I read more. I walked more. I forced myself to do all of the things I never let myself or was scared to do alone. I had to. I was alone, after all.

The more I learned, grew, and grieved, I learned I wasn't alone. Sometimes it really did feel like I was, but I had developed a community... just in nontraditional ways. I had family, but I needed to let go of the anger I held. I had friends who loved me, but I needed to let myself be loved.

None of this came easy. Writing it in words makes it seem like having a baby, suffering with PPD, and not having support isn't the end of the world. But that's not the truth. It was and will probably continue to be one of the hardest things I'll endure in my lifetime. I was lost for a long time, and the thought that I missed out on such great moments with my daughter in her first year of life due to being so sick and so unwell pains me. I still struggle with that thought. But something in me during those hardest times of my life forced me to figure it out. I had my daughter, I had me, and I needed to give my daughter something better than the me that was being this way every day. I knew she deserved to see her mother smile and laugh with her. I knew she deserved to have a good relationship with her father and his family and not miss out on any of those moments they could provide her. That doesn't mean it didn't hurt and wasn't painful. It just means I knew I needed to try. For her, and then for me.

I'm here to tell my story because I know there's others in my same situation. I know the lack of support for mothers, and I know forcing ourselves to get better isn't the easiest step, but I am also here to tell you how worth it this fight is and how worth it it is to get yourself better for the ones you love. I'm here to remind you that in the depths of the grief, pain, and hurt that you are important and needed, and it will not always feel this way.

Motherhood is a ride. Some of my chapters feel dark while others have so much light shone into them, you'd go blind.

Chapter 16
URSULA ERASMUS
www.mygempower.com | @mygempower

I already knew when I reached my sweet sixteen that I would get married and have kids. The expectation was clear; the adoption, almost universal. That is, unless you were "different." No one ever spoke about what "different" really meant, but I had been indoctrinated enough to know without question that "different" was also labeled difficult, outsider, odd, and a whole string of other adjectives. I didn't want to be on the wrong side of acceptable. I was programmed to please. So I followed the universal pattern. Clearly, I qualified for motherhood. I was female, after all. And all of my mom's female relatives and contemporaries thought I'd be super qualified because my mom had been a children's nanny in England. Even some of my friends thought I was lucky because my mom would know all the answers. And then some.

Before I reached my teens, though, things had come undone. By the time I was 10 years old, my family unit, my safe space in early childhood, had dramatically changed. My older siblings had departed the nest. My dad had also flown. There were no explanations offered; therefore, I thought my situation was both strange and scary. Until that point, I thought my family was very ordinary. Then, all of a sudden, my brain was scrambled by all the taboo topics and secrecy. I felt abandoned and overwhelmed. The world was big and scary and did not make sense. I was hoping that a parent or someone would show up and show me how to navigate day to day.

Instead, my pre-teen, lonely brain was desperately trying to make sense of things. I remember thinking that all of the disruption and messed-up stuff I was observing in the adults around me qualified me to be considered a grown-up. I had to get a handle on that shit. I mean, I'd had "conversations" with my mom about how there would be no money from my dad (not true, ultimately); she would get a job, and the two of us would be living in a new area. And a very different lifestyle. This didn't feel like regular 10-year-old stuff to me. The little bit of rebel in me was determined to survive the remaining years of school so that I could blossom, be proud of my accomplishments, and fulfill my role: marriage and motherhood. And so for 8 years, it was one day at a time, through the highs and lows of living with a mother struggling with depression.

I married at 19 by my own free will. I was not pregnant. But I was determined to get on with the show. Although back in 1980, I had to have both my parents sign a Permission To Marry document for the courts. The requisite dash of drama emerged. Of course, my dad signed first, angering my mom. Eventually, I was free to unfurl my wings and fly the coop. There had been no conversations about marriage or relationships. Nada. Oh, and I had also attended an all-girls Catholic school, where we discussed obeying our parents and our relationship with God. That's a slim and almost useless focus for the bigness of life. All I knew about my new role and stage of life was what I had experienced in my childhood. And a few snippets from the domestic situations of friends I had sleepovers with. All Catholic families. Not much variety to learn from. Suck it up, buttercup!

Immediately after marrying, we went to live in Germany for 3 years. Those were the good days where I could try and figure out what I had come through. I loved the freedom to break out of all the habits I had been raised with. It felt cathartic and reinforced my belief that I was absolutely ready and prepared for the next chapter. My 60-something self knows now that at that time, I was viewing my life from birth to age 19 like watching a movie. Without a guide or the ability to deeply reflect, it was not a super helpful experience. Interesting, yes. Hard to process alone, yes. There were tears, anger aplenty, and still the sense that I had been abandoned. Real understanding had not yet shown up. I would have been an outstanding "project" for a therapist at that time.

I really, really wanted to stake a claim on my happily ever after and prove to the world (and to myself) that I was able to create a new blueprint. I had my first baby at 22 and the second at 25. What on Earth did I know about anything?! When I read these words now, I actually laugh out loud and cringe a little. At the time, I thought I was so ready, so capable, and so competent to make a secure home for myself and my babes. Everything in my background had prepared me to marry and have a family. Motherhood was always the central achievement. And I was expected to ace it all. I put one foot in front of the other, fueled by coffee, and ignored the parts of my history that had wounded and confused my inner child.

I am Gucci Erasmus, and this is my story.

My account of motherhood, when I look back on those years, is a mix of humour, absurdity, and terror. I don't know where or when the actual beginning of my awakening and awareness occurred, but there I was not fully raised myself, and yet I was raising two humans. It probably wasn't a single moment but more like a series of painful prods from my inner child to try and make me pay attention. There were also the numerous times I was told that I didn't know what I was doing. Funnily, it's true. I did not know what I was doing. But in all that I was doing, I was just following the rules, standards, and beliefs of the day—apart from the teeny slivers of rebellion.

Pregnancy was neither unpleasant nor glorious for me, aside from the awful fashions that had me imitating a hot air balloon on some days or a Squishmallow on others. I ultimately had two c-sections, one unplanned and one semi-planned, as they were quite common in the 1980s.

Women had been socially primed to want zero damage to their parts in exchange for their labour of love in carrying a babe, so we were happy to skip the actual labour. Looking back, I'm amazed that there was no conversation about the physical and mental impact of birth. My OBGYN basically told me that my husband (and he added, as I recall, any future husbands) would thank me for my choice of c-section. The prevailing message to women: a perfect body was a condition of love. Planned birth simply made it easier for the men in my life to stick to their work week or weekend plans. I vividly recall thinking that I was not prepared to negotiate or make my own needs clear. This was a tiny bit of an awakening. With the wisdom of hindsight, I know that this was not a choice at all. I did not realize I had agency or a voice. I was young and a pleaser, just like most of the women in my circle during those years.

So there I was at home with a pair of cute kids, following advice from both my own mom and the book every mama had at that time, written by a wonderful woman called Marina. She was the maven of baby and child care. I think she really wanted to support women and simplify things. Her advice was practical. I had those little sticky page markers all over that book. I embraced all the advice sandwiched in those pages. Then there were all the women's magazines, each with its own column on parenting. Although, if I recall, there was very little reference to dads in any of it. Parenting was primarily the domain of the mama bear in the early years. Those columns were full of "how-to" tips and clear "standards" for good parenting. I was always clipping and saving those columns so that I could reread them and make sure to get this stuff right, especially the ideas around creating the right environment at home. In one word: TIDY. I am cursed by being organized and tidy, so this felt easy for me. I was always creeping around between 11pm and midnight putting things back in place (and I mean the *exact* spot) so we would be good to go the next day. All of this made me secretly frustrated but weirdly elated because I was doing the right thing. Underneath all of this focus on appearance, I faced daily battles of willpower with my kids. I didn't understand the balance between freedom and good habits. Yes, I was wound up tight like a spring.

The littles were always looking cute, the house was always clean and tidy, and the meals were always good. I managed to quickly shrink myself down to return to a pre-baby body. I was chasing the gold standard. I wanted to please everyone. But I never thought for a moment that I deserved to be considered. I was emotionally overwhelmed, and I thought no one would understand. I put one foot in front of the other, day by day, through the infant and toddler years, wearing my best smile and a pair of jeans I bought in the teen department. You get the picture...

The realization did not hit me at any particular point in time that there was something else going on beneath the surface of my day-to-day routine with my babies. I didn't wake up one morning and look in the mirror and admit to myself that I had great big voids to fill or emotional mountains to climb. No, it was not like that. I couldn't see where the fuck-ups ahead would be. It slowly dawned on me that I was operating from a place of fear, shame, and guilt quite a lot of the time. When those realizations started to accumulate, the awareness hit me as though I had been hit by an icy blast of Arctic air. I immediately began to see where I was both comparing myself to other mamas and trying to keep up. I relentlessly judged myself. I was caught up in living my life according to the ideas of others. Do you know that being scared and angry affects the way you relate to your children? I do.

There is one universal desire I have heard spoken by every mama who crossed my path, and this was my desire, too. I really wanted to raise kids who took responsibility for their actions. My frame of reference for this desire back then was that my son would be a good man and more empathic than the men who came before him and my daughter would be a good woman and more adventurous than the women of earlier generations. To be honest, it was almost impossible for me to consider that my kids could be rebels and rule breakers but still be responsible. Can we break out of the mold and still be responsible? My childhood had not been a place where I could make a mistake and be allowed to learn from it, so I could move on with an ever larger understanding of how to be me.

Can you believe it that on confession days at the school I attended, I was encouraged to make up something to confess if I mentioned to my class teacher that I didn't need to join the snaking lineup to the chapel? The rebel in me wanted to confess to lying so that I had something to confess, but the good girl in me won the debate every time, and I never opened my mouth! I was oppressed by fear and punishment. I really couldn't model what it looked like to be responsible and acknowledge that my choices may have had negative consequences. This makes me cringe. I mean, it sounds so stupid now when I think about it. Whose script was I living? Whose BS was I serving up for my kids?

My children starting kindergarten was a breakout experience for me. Meeting new mamas and kids meant some new beliefs were popping up between the same old shit. Instead of a run-of-the-mill book club, five of us mamas started a champagne breakfast club. It sounds so glamorous, and in truth, it was one of the best things to bless my life. We felt so badass. We should have had matching tattoos! Two of those women are my friends to this day, 35 years on. We talked about everything in our club—all those taboo and risky topics that we didn't let into our conversations with our partners or our mothers. We had just one glass of champagne a piece at each brunch, a litany of conversations, lots of laughter, and buckets of tears.

My lesson from this is that women need friends who will get into the gritty stuff. I think this is a special category of friend, a friend who is radically honest with herself and with you. It is such a wonderful gift to have a friend who will listen with an open heart and mind and a friend who will debate and sometimes agree to disagree. This space to connect was such a big part of me learning that it was both okay and necessary to raise myself and that it is reasonable to do this while raising your own offspring. If you don't have a friend like this, you need one—someone who is compassionate and who takes you as you are.

There is another lesson from the kindergarten years that I have to recount: the nativity play and Christmas concert. My daughter had the most amazing waist-length hair that was shot with gold and titian. The teachers wanted her to play the part of the angel Gabriel. One of the moms made her a white satin angel dress. She learned her lines and practiced them over and over. We braided her hair the night before the concert, and she slept on all those thick ropes of hair. The nativity play was lovely. She delivered her lines and looked angelic. Families enjoyed the hotdogs and potluck.

Eventually, we headed home. In the car, my littlest was quietly sobbing. When I enquired, she told me she was "... very angry because you made me be a boy, Mummy." My first reaction was to laugh. How insensitive. Then she told me that somebody's big brother had told her Gabriel was a boy. I ranted right there in front of my kids, judging the other child and saying that his parents would be sorry. I didn't stop to check my emotions; therefore, I couldn't be trusted by my own littles. The lesson from this incident took a while to emerge for me. I had been dismissed so many times myself during my childhood that I was stuck there. We still talk about this when we reminisce about those years.

When my son entered Grade 1, we got two rabbits. If you have ever had multiple rodents or bunnies, you might be snickering right now. This was a responsibility project. The bunbuns had a lovely hutch in the back garden. The kids did the feeding every day, and they helped with cleaning out for our two fluffy friends. We didn't see too much of the bunnies. They'd dug a little burrow and occasionally popped out for a juicy carrot. One morning, my son rushed into the kitchen breathless and with eyes like saucers. He was out of breath, but he didn't appear traumatized. I think I had said "what's up in the garden?" He looked me dead in the eye and said, "There are bunnies all over the hutch. Lots and lots." I must have given him a disbelieving look because the next thing out of his mouth was "What will you give me if I am right?"

That right there was one of those *bam*, slap-in-face moments for me. Absolute clarity. My son didn't feel heard or believed, and so he had to add a condition to our exchange. That was the day I shifted my commitment to try and be much more open to trusting my kids. I was not always able to do this, not by a long shot. Remember, I was the girl who was encouraged to lie to go to confession.

There was so much fear for me to overcome that I would go out of my way to avoid having to talk about or acknowledge where I had messed up. It is no surprise to me that I was so masterful at suppressing every detail of what I messed up that I can barely recall the details of those situations. But sure as hell, I can still connect to the feelings. Those feelings are like tattoos that I can mostly keep hidden, tattoos that I regret acquiring but that I can attend to and remind myself that I have come a long way.

There's a Tibetan saying that I really like. It goes like this: "Bless those who curse and revile you, for they shall be your greatest teachers."

You probably already know this, but kids see through everything. Mine had little brain lasers to know when I was not being honest. They also had little heart lasers to know when I was afraid or when I felt guilt or any way in which I was oppressed by the bullshit I had been gifted by culture, family, and even friends. My two used to sniff out my irrational behaviour from a mile off. They tested my boundaries when they saw that I didn't care about boundaries for myself. They also played small at times, shrinking back from their essence to reflect more of my default behaviour. My behaviour must have seemed so hypocritical and confusing to them. Luckily, they never said "get that crazy lady outta here." They gave me so much leeway and were very forgiving. But they did describe me as weird and even as a drag-on on different occasions. In middle school, my daughter introduced me as her dragon a few times. At least by that time, I had begun to listen and sit with things before reacting. Mostly. This is actually a lifetime practice I have since learned.

I was in traffic one day when I realized that the man in the car beside me was peering at me with a puzzled expression. I think I gave him the finger. Or maybe I laughed because I knew he wouldn't get it. I was smack dab in the middle of one of those conversations with myself. You know the big serious conversations that can get quite loud in your head. It is possible that I was talking out loud or possibly talking to two little people strapped into the car seats in the backseat. It is scary to think about those listening ears taking in my messages that were never meant for them. Sorry, kids.

The thing about those conversations with myself that I find fascinating is sometimes they were brutally honest, and yet they didn't lead to any action until a decade later.

I just suppressed what I really knew in my heart of hearts I should do. I ignored the actions I knew I should take because I didn't feel like I had the permission or the capability. Other times, those conversations were like fake news. Who was I trying to kid? Was I trying to convince myself that I was doing OK and everything would work out well? Did I swallow some kind of cultural nonsense?

The bottom line is that I was not being true to myself. I lost count how many times I was walking someone else's walk or talking someone else's talk. There's a litany of mistakes associated with walking someone else's walk. These standards and beliefs that often had no correlation with the woman I hoped to be were what I was generously gifting to my children. In retrospect, this is the most painful part of not consciously knowing that I needed to safely nurture and raise myself. I just wish the movie *Because I Said So* had come out years earlier. It is a favourite that I watch with my daughter every Christmas time, with much shared laughter. "Because I said so" should never be the answer to any situation unless lives are in danger.

This is my "because I said so" list from those years:

- Children needed to eat everything that was put on their plate
- Children only got a dessert or treat when they had eaten everything else
- Girls wore dresses to church and parties
- Girls were not allowed to climb trees in their nice clothes
- Boys needed to have a short, conservative haircut
- Boys couldn't go out with anything that had a hole or a rip in it (same for girls)
- Tantrums were verboten
- Speaking back was verboten
- Greeting adults involved hugs and kisses

- Whooping it up indoors was not allowed
- (At least we didn't have the don't speak unless spoken to rule)
- Friends must be suitable
- Play must be contained in the spaces for play (My kids will remember countless other rules that I have forgotten)
- Santa's naughty or nice framework determined if the kids got presents or treats

(Where does The Elf on the Shelf fit?)

You might be interested to know that in the 1980s, when I became a mom, the prevailing narrative around behaviour was that if needed, you could scare or manipulate your children into compliance; and as a last resort, you could bribe them into compliance. It's interesting because your mama might have been raised under those beliefs, too.

Raising myself as a bit of a late starter, it is fascinating to me that although I didn't encourage my kids to have their own points of view and to think about values and beliefs and consider what they really liked, somehow they figured it out. My offspring learned to hold opinions and determine for themselves what was really important. The gap. What type of tools and conversations are appropriate to engage others with your unique points of view? Well, hell. I had no idea.

Like probably every other mother out there, I've joked about how much my kids would have to spend on therapy to be fully repaired and put back together after being bothered by me. Despite when I yelled and words I regret flew out of my mouth or when I was irrational or didn't listen, they still laughed at some of my craziest ideas until we all had tears of laughter gushing down our faces. They were tender when I needed that, too. I hugged them tight.

During those crazy years of childhood (theirs, not mine), I really didn't know anything about soothing myself. Self-care was not in my vernacular. I didn't have a clue about getting back to a stable place; however, intuition was my powerful guide. Sitting in a sunny spot in the garden with the youngsters charging through the sprinkler, taking a cozy 15 minutes to journal, and even recording my dreams upon waking—all these are good things. They helped me to stop reacting and instead respond mindfully. And so the wheel turned, across phases and decades and countries. Change was/is constant. And learning, too, if I remember to let it in.

Around the time I reached a half century on this Earth, celebrating the big 50, I figured out that my greatest teachers were, in fact, my kids. Right then, I also understood that I had raised myself while I was raising my kids. Until we got to kindergarten, I was managing to live the good girl, ignorant, and small life that ruffled few feathers. Then my rebellion started in small ways: to prioritize fun, not to follow blindly, and to ask for help occasionally. I don't get a do-over, but I can be a cycle-breaking grandmother. That's my plan.

Chapter 17
VANESSA DA PONTE
@vane0218

Survival...

If I had to use one word to describe 2020, that would be it. Survival. The year 2020 was the beginning of my journey into motherhood. If only I could have told the younger me who always wanted to be a mother just how difficult this ride was going to be...

My name is Vanessa. I am a mom of 2 boys, and I've been wanting to share my story in hopes that it can help someone else in theirs.

January 11th, 2020, I gave birth to a beautiful little boy. Today, I can look back and say it was one of the best days of my life because of this little guy—but, let's be honest, labour/giving birth is hard and connecting with this tiny human doesn't always happen instantly. But gosh, I love him. As we all know, March 2020 was the start of something awful and so hard as a first-time mom. It was not at all what I envisioned my maternity leave to be like, but we made the most of our time together at home, this little boy and his momma. My husband and I knew we wanted to have children close in age, so as soon as we had the green light, we started trying for baby number 2. In May 2020, I found out I was pregnant. We were very happy, but wow that was quick!

Soon after is where things started to get difficult. I was very sick with nausea, vomiting, and migraines, I couldn't sleep, and I could barely take care of myself, let alone my almost 5 month old and the little baby growing inside of me. I remember always saying, "If my first pregnancy was like this, I would not have had more kids!" The struggle was so real, and I had no clue what else to do. Regardless of the pandemic, I needed help. I needed my family to help me through because I became incapable of being home alone with my baby. Everyone was worried. They thought I was dealing with postpartum depression; I just wanted to lay on the couch and barely move unless I needed to use the bathroom, and even that was a struggle. "What kind of mother am I?" I used to ask myself this question over and over. Why couldn't I take care of my baby? Why wasn't I able to be the mother I always thought I would be? This second pregnancy was kicking my butt and giving me the worst mom guilt ever. I kept wondering if we made the right decision in having children so close together.

After my 12-week appointment with my OB, I was given medication to help with the nausea, but that didn't work. I called her office and tried to get another appointment because nothing was helping. My husband was a huge support system, but man was he scared. He showed up at the OB's office to try and get someone to see me again and explain that something was severely wrong. "I'm sorry, sir. She will have to wait for her next appointment" was the response he received. We went to the ER, and I was told to stop the medication, but there was nothing else to do but wait it out because I was "pregnant, in my first trimester, and all my symptoms were very common for that stage." I was tired. And tired of being tired. I was also tired of hearing, "You're pregnant. It's normal." This wasn't normal. I hated what I was feeling. I hated how this pregnancy made me feel so crappy (and that also made me feel guilty). I hated not being able to care for my baby boy who was growing oh so quickly. I hated all of it to the point where I started to hate myself. Why was my body doing this to me at a time where I needed to be the best version of myself for my family? I felt like a failure, like my body was letting me and my family down in every way possible.

There were so many nights where I was awake, and I felt like I was living a nightmare! While my husband and son were sleeping, I would toss and turn, get up, lay on the ceramic floor in my bathroom to cool my body down, get up again, go sit on the couch and try to sleep sitting up, cry and scream for how much pain I was in, and do that over and over again until morning would come, and nothing would change aside from the fact that I was one day closer to that second trimester. How many nights would my husband care for our son because I just wasn't able to do anything? Why was this happening to me? This little baby just needed some comfort every now and then, and I couldn't give it to him. The combination of early motherhood and pregnancy was NOT working for me.

I felt empty. I felt so much pain yet so numb at the same time. There was no way to describe the amount of physical pain I felt in my head or how guilty I felt for not being present for my son. I was there physically, but mentally I couldn't be. No one could understand what was happening, and it wasn't their fault; even I had no idea what was happening. They would try to snap me out of it: "Vane, come on. Get it together!" I would hear them, but I had no clue how to get it together. It was almost like an out-of-body experience. I could see myself and the look on my face. It was a blank stare. I was empty inside.

August 12th, 2020, after visiting my optometrist for an emergency appointment because my vision started changing (I was seeing double), I was told I needed to leave their office and go straight to the hospital ER. "UM, WHAT?!" I had left my 7-month-old son at my parents' house so I could go to this appointment and get it fixed or be told it would get better in a few days, and now I needed to go to the ER?! It seemed very serious. I felt so many emotions, and I was kind of in denial. How did I leave my baby with my mom during nap time just to go to this appointment that would "fix me," and now we're heading to the ER? My husband picked me up, we went straight to the hospital, and I was seen soon after. After multiple tests and scans, I was brought to a bed to wait for the results, so I knew I wasn't leaving any time soon. When the doctor came to see us, I saw her face, and I could tell that this wasn't going to be good. And then the words came out of her mouth. "Miss Da Ponte, the scans show that you have a tumour between your brain and cerebellum. You need emergency surgery to remove it, and you will be transferred to the CHUM (Centre Hospitalier de l'Université de Montréal), as they have the best neuro team in Montreal, either tonight or tomorrow morning." I can't say I was shocked, but I think I was in a state of shock, if that makes any sense. I just wanted to go home and see my baby boy, but that wasn't possible. I needed to stay at the hospital and be transferred by ambulance because at any moment, my condition could have changed. I was walking, talking, eating, and moving around with no issues, but at any moment, that could have all changed. I knew I was safer in the hospital than if I had gone home. As much as I wanted to hug and kiss my sweet little boy, I knew I needed to be here.

Then the next thought came to my mind, and I said, "I'm 14 weeks pregnant. I haven't eaten since lunch. Can I have something to eat?" she responded, "Your husband better go grab you something to eat now because as of midnight, you can't eat in case you have surgery tomorrow." So off he went to buy me a soup and a sandwich. I was lying there alone, and all I could think was "I'm scared." It had finally hit me. I called my older sister and gave her the news. I cried. She cried. I shared my fears, and I told her I loved her. At that moment, I wanted to call everyone I knew, especially my parents who were home with my baby boy, but I couldn't find it in me to do so. It was so late, and I knew they were waiting for news, but they were probably asleep. And who would want to wake up to THIS kind of news in the middle of the night? So I figured I'd let them sleep. We'll tell them tomorrow morning.

My husband returned with my food, and even with his mask on, I could see he'd had his moment of fear, too. His eyes had just shed some tears, and he was trying to keep a brave face. That's the kind of person he is. In the last 7 years, I've seen him cry twice. He was and continues to be my rock through it all. I couldn't have asked for a better person to be by my side while all this craziness was happening. Soon after, I was transferred to the CHUM, where I stayed alone for almost 24 hours because of, well, you know, the pandemic. That was probably the hardest part, being alone with the worst news I had ever received. The neurosurgeon came to speak to me, and I suddenly felt a little better. He was calm and assured me that although this was very scary for me, after looking at my scans, he'd determined that it was a simple procedure for him to remove this tumour. He felt confident but did mention that this would be his first time performing this "routine procedure" on a pregnant woman. But sadly, I didn't have a say. I needed this surgery. There was no other way to save me. Cue some more mom guilt. This surgery would help keep me alive but may kill my baby? What do you do? There wasn't a choice. I had to think of my son who was waiting for me at home. He needed me, and I needed him, too.

After my "vid" test came back negative, I was told my husband could come back, and I was transferred to the ICU because I needed a nurse available 24 hours a day, not because I couldn't do anything, but because I needed neuro exams done every 10 minutes to assure my state hadn't changed. I was doing well. I was on medication to relieve the pressure I was feeling in my head. I was eating better. I was sleeping. But the only downside was I couldn't see my family, baby boy included. He was growing so fast, and I was missing him so much. I was so grateful to have my family watch over him while I couldn't be there, but man, the mom guilt was so real. I wasn't there for him, and now I needed a surgery that could possibly cost me the little baby inside me. I hated the position I was in, but I kept telling myself that I didn't have a choice. I needed the surgery if I wanted to live a somewhat normal life and be a mom for the little boy I already had, the boy who already knew his mom.

My husband was spending most of the visitor's hours with me and then going home to our son. A few days in, and a few audiobooks and podcasts later, we finally got the news: August 18th, 2020 was going to be my surgery day! WOOHOO!! Awesome! I looked over to my husband and said, "You're going to have to shave my legs!" Being the woman I am, I felt so uncomfortable that I wasn't groomed for this surgery. Crazy, right? It was the least of my worries days prior, but now that the meds were helping with the pain, reality kicked in. I needed to shave! He laughed and thought I was crazy, but let me tell you, it was one of our best and funniest moments together. My sister delivered a little care package, and my husband set up our own little bathroom section in my little ICU room. There was no actual bathroom because most ICU patients aren't in a state to get up alone to use the bathroom, so there was just a sink. He set up a chair and some towels and started shaving my legs. Gosh, it was so funny but also a clear indication that I married the right person. No judgement. I mean, he did think I was a little crazy, and it was hilarious that I was going to have an 8-hour brain surgery, but my main thought was SHAVING MY DAMN LEGS!

On surgery day, I remember waking up and feeling great. I was one step closer to recovery and seeing my boy! I knew that day I had a war to fight, but I had the best soldiers behind me. I kissed my husband goodbye that morning at 6:30am, and I was wheeled off to pre-op. I felt cool, calm, and collected. I was so calm that my anesthesiologist asked, "You do know you're about to undergo an 8-hour brain surgery, right?!" YES. Of course!!! But there was no reason to be nervous or stressed because the next part was completely out of my hands. Why stress over something I have zero control over? I gave my neurosurgeon all my confidence. He would save me. I just had to go to sleep for a few hours, wake up, and it would all be over.

I did wake up, hours and hours later. I opened my eyes, and I was told everything went well. The tumour was out and sent for a biopsy, and I got to hear my baby's heartbeat. He was there with me the whole time. He was alive. We did it! My husband stayed until visiting hours were over and gave everyone the news that I was out of surgery and everything went well. The next few hours were tough and critical for the baby, though. As for me, I was sleeping on and off and really wanted to avoid any pain medication unless I absolutely couldn't stand the pain. I was thinking like a mom again. Doctors came in on a daily basis to check the baby's heartbeat to make sure everything was okay and that he was still pushing through this critical stage. Every time they came in, I felt like my heart had stopped until the second we heard his strong, little heart beating, and then everything felt better instantly. They felt like the longest two-to-five minutes of my life!

They'd put a drain in my head, so the doctors could see how much liquid was still in my head. That was SO annoying! Walking around and sitting down, I was in constant fear that I would trip over or sit on this drain, and it would fly right out. But it was part of the process. Once that drain came out, I'd be that much closer to going home. After 3 days, they closed the drain, and that was the big test. If I didn't feel pressure in my head, the drain would be officially removed. But if I did, they would have to open it again. Day after day, I would wake up and think, "Is today the day I can get rid of this damn drain?" Well, that day finally came, and let me tell you... getting that drain out—OUCH! But it meant I was one step closer.

Recovery after the drain wasn't as hard, but it was still challenging getting my balance back, walking without holding onto anything, and wearing my glasses again. I wanted to get moving as quickly as possible. I wanted out of this place. They were all so good to me, but I wanted to go home and see my baby. When we got the news that I was able to go home (no cancer, no physio, or anything), I just couldn't believe this part was over. Yes, I still had a long road of recovery ahead, but I would be at home. I'd be a "normal" pregnant woman and mother just living a regular life!

I got out of that hospital gown, put on some regular clothes, and for the first time, I rubbed my pregnant belly, and it finally felt so good. I waited anxiously for my husband to pick me up. When I saw him walk through the door, I was overjoyed! We headed towards the car and drove to my parents' house where we would be staying for the next couple of months, as I still needed to be extremely careful, and I did have over 30 stitches and 10 staples in my head. I was so happy to see part of my family; we had dinner, and I finally felt like a somewhat normal pregnant woman. I was hungry. I could eat and actually enjoy it. This was THE BEST dinner EVER! I was able to talk to my family and not want to hide from everyone. It was glorious! And reuniting with my son... WOW that was priceless. No words could describe that moment! After only seeing me through a phone screen for weeks, when we finally reunited, he couldn't stop touching my face. It was almost as if he couldn't believe I was actually in front of him. He was not quite 8 months old, so Mommy missing a few weeks of his little life was a lot for him and for me.

What was next for me? My pregnancy was now considered high risk. I needed a lot of therapy to heal from the mental aspect of all this. My physical recovery was the easier part. Therapy was my best friend. I needed to voice my feelings and thoughts because the after effect of all this was quite a heavy load to carry. And given the pandemic, I was limited on who I could see. As much as I wanted to hug every person I knew and share this awful part of my life to gain some closure, I couldn't. It's almost as if I had to pretend it didn't even happen. Luckily, I was able to consult with professionals because I felt very disconnected from my son. I was no longer his person for comfort, and it broke me. My therapist told me, "Give it time. The bond will come back. He will trust you again." It was probably the hardest part of our reunion and my recovery. I wanted to be the person he came to when he was hurt, when he was scared, or when he wanted to simply cuddle. And right now, I wasn't. As much as I was extremely grateful for my family being there for him when I couldn't be, I couldn't stop thinking "now he doesn't want or love me." I needed our bond to get back to what it was before his little brother was born because I was so afraid that if it didn't, he would see me with his brother and really feel as though he was replaced.

Motherhood is such a crazy thing! It isn't easy whether you're a stay-at-home mom or a working mom. It's hard. As my husband likes to say, we are the glue that keeps the family together. Moms take care of groceries, cleaning, cooking, play dates, family activities, vacations, laundry, husbands (that's another story for another time), and the list goes on and on. It's the job that requires the most time and patience, but you don't always get the recognition. And now my kid wants nothing to do with me. Great, another round of mom guilt! After quite a few months and lots of bonding, I regained his trust. We were our little dynamic duo again. I was so grateful.

My next challenge was loneliness. How was I surrounded by family yet I felt so alone? Why is this happening to me? I should feel happy. I survived. I am here with my son. I made it. We made it. It was all I ever wanted while in the hospital, and now that I had it, I questioned everything. I needed to know why I survived what had just happened to me. Without knowing that answer, I felt like I'd lost myself, and I couldn't just be happy with the response,

"I was one of the lucky ones."

Don't get me wrong, I was grateful, and I still am, but I was also so lost. It was a real rollercoaster of emotions, and even to this day, I still struggle with it. I know I survived to be a mother for my boys, but there must be something more. Something changed; something inside of me couldn't stop searching. It isn't an easy journey even after all this. I still have so many questions, but I am working on myself and trying to find those answers. One thing is for sure: I know I needed to share this story, even if it only helps one person out there who is going through a difficult time, and even if their story isn't identical to mine. Maybe that's my purpose.

Most of the time, when people hear my story, they say, "Vanessa, you're so strong. I wouldn't have been able to go through all that." Yes, I am strong. I am a daughter, a sister, a wife, and a mother. And thanks to my children, I am alive. They gave me strength I didn't know I had, and I am so lucky to be their mom. Today, I can look back on this horrible experience, and I am able to say that although it was scary, I never thought of dying. Weird, but so true. I was struggling to the point where I would even forget I was pregnant, but now I look back, and I almost judge myself. "How could I not remember this little guy growing inside me?" Now that we've made it through, and I was able to give birth to my second child, I look back and say, "How could I almost allow myself to lose him?" It's a crazy feeling because after 2 years, I know him, and I can't imagine my life without him. But when all this was happening, I sometimes almost forgot he was there. The weird part is that although I would often forget he was there through the struggle, we created a unique bond. And that's something I could never fully put into words. This little boy was literally with me every step of the way, when so many couldn't be there with me at all.

I may not have all the answers; I definitely don't have all the ones I am still looking for, but what I do know is as moms, we forget how to care for ourselves. But if we want to be the best moms, we NEED to care for ourselves. We need to stand up for ourselves and not let anyone tell us how or what we should feel. We need to support one another because we are not alone, regardless of what we go through. We need to share our stories because they will help someone. It can change a life. I know that it could have changed mine, and I would have felt a little less alone. We often settle for "it's a normal part of pregnancy" or any suggestions a doctor makes, but sometimes we need to advocate for ourselves. That second opinion can change a life. You can find out something scary, but you can also save yourself like I did. If I had just accepted that my vision was simply "messed up" and waited for my next OB appointment, what then? Would I be here today? Would I have survived this nightmare? Would I be able to walk or talk? Trust your gut, never settle, and always put yourself first! And don't feel bad for doing it. It'll only mean that you'll be there for the ones you love.

Survival. 2020, I was in survival mode, but I made it through. It wasn't easy. It still isn't, but I'm here to share my story. This story isn't meant to be about how beautiful motherhood is. It can be, but it's also about how motherhood has a ton of challenges, and sometimes, it's about survival. The good news is it gets better, and you start living.

If you're a mom that is struggling in any way, shape, or form, just know that you are never alone.

"Being a mother is learning about strengths you didn't know you had and dealing with fears you didn't know existed." — Nishan Panwar

Publisher's Note
COURTNEY ST. CROIX
Leadherpublishing.com | IG: @leadherpublishing

It is such an honour and a privilege to be able to support independent writers as they share their stories with us in a collaborative book project. I have seen Amanda open up important dialogues about motherhood within her platform *Honest as a Mother*, and this book series serves as yet another way moms can have a place to openly discuss their experiences through a lifelong journey of growth and learning, without judgement, shame, or fear.

I started hosting group book projects initially on the topic of self-love, because I knew I had some things to say about my own self-love journey, but I also inherently knew that there was **so much value** to sharing a multitude of different perspectives on the topic, outside of just my own.

The power of multiple voices coming together as one is incredible, and I am so grateful for and proud of each of the authors inside this book who has chosen to share her story with the world. We need to hear your voices, even more than you know.

If you are interested in joining a group book project in the future, be sure to check out leadherpublishing.com for co-author program details and upcoming projects.

And, if you're a coach or industry leader looking to lead and facilitate a collaborative book of your own, I'd love to hear more about your topic and discuss the potential for joining the LeadHer Publishing team as a Lead Author.

Thank you for reading!

Courtney St Croix
Founder, LeadHer Publishing

To find out more about LeadHer Publishing's books,
services, and collaborative projects, visit leadherpublishing.com

www.ingramcontent.com/pod-product-compliance
Lightning Source LLC
Chambersburg PA
CBHW051001140626
46546CB00017B/2116